CAST IRON RECIPES

The Ultimate Cast Iron Cookbook With More Then Delicious Recipes

(The Easy Dutch Oven Cookbook With More Than Cozy Recipes)

Thomas Hicks

Published by Sharon Lohan

© Thomas Hicks

All Rights Reserved

Cast Iron Recipes: The Ultimate Cast Iron Cookbook With More Then Delicious Recipes (The Easy Dutch Oven Cookbook With More Than Cozy Recipes)

ISBN 978-1-990334-97-9

All rights reserved. No part of this guide may be reproduced in any form without permission in writing from the publisher except in the case of brief quotations embodied in critical articles or reviews.

Legal & Disclaimer

The information contained in this book is not designed to replace or take the place of any form of medicine or professional medical advice. The information in this book has been provided for educational and entertainment purposes only.

The information contained in this book has been compiled from sources deemed reliable, and it is accurate to the best of the Author's knowledge; however, the Author cannot guarantee its accuracy and validity and cannot be held liable for any errors or omissions. Changes are periodically made to this book. You must consult your doctor or get professional medical advice before using any of the suggested remedies, techniques, or information in this book.

Table of contents

Part 1 1

Recipe 1: Tasty Chicken Enchilada Skillet 2

Recipe 2: Sour Cream Style Cornbread 4

Recipe 3: Easy Sunday Skillet Breakfast 6

Recipe 4: Pork Chops In Pepper And Jelly Sauce 8

Recipe 5: Easy Scalloped Potatoes 11

Recipe 6: Wild Rice And Chicken Casserole 13

Recipe 7: Pecan Fried Catfish 16

Recipe 8: Kale And Potato Frittata 18

Recipe 9: Hearty Sweet Potato Salad 20

Recipe 10: Cast Iron Skillet Style Salsa 22

Recipe 11: Fruit Packed Pancakes 24

Recipe 12: Sweet Potato Onion Cakes 26

Recipe 13: Succulent Filet Mignon 28

Recipe 14: Smoked Trout With Apple Hash 30

Recipe 15: Cornbread Style Focaccia 33

Recipe 16: Charred Peppers With Dipping Sauce 35

Recipe 17: Hearty Fried Tomatoes 37

Recipe 18: Blistered Brussel Sprouts 39

Recipe 19: Pork Style Quesadillas 41

Recipe 20: Braised Turnips 43

Recipe 21: Sweet Tasting Apricot Cinnamon Rolls 45

Recipe 22: Apple And Cinnamon "Pancake" 47

Recipe 23: Pecan Fried Okra 50

Recipe 24: Wholesome Top Shelf Baked Chicken 52

Recipe 25: Upside Down Pineapple And Carrot Cake 55

Part 2 57

Breakfast 58

Carrot-Zucchini-Nut Muffins 58

Mountain Man Breakfast 59

Johnna's Ham And Cheese Cornbread 59

Full Count Cornbread 60

Upside Down Salsa Cornbread 62

Skillet Cornbread 63

Mexican Cornbread 64

Fall Run Jalapeno Cornbread 64

Peach Upside Down Cake 65

Pineapple Upside Down Cake 66

Cornbread 66

Grandma Charlotte's Black Magic Corn Bread 67

Fancy West Virginia Cornbread 68

My Crusty Cornbread 69

Wv Skillet Upside Down Cake 69

Raspberry Skillet Cake	70
Spiced Pear Skillet Cake	71
Meat (Beef, Pork, Lamb)	73
Beef Fajitas	73
Iron Skillet Ramps And Bacon	73
Spiced Pork Tenderloin With Sautéed Apples	74
Easy Beef Stew	75
Coalminer's Pie	76
Bacon And Pimento Cheese Pizza	77
Kenny's Country Gravy	78
Skillet S'mores Dip	79
Thick Cut Salt & Pepper Pork Chops	80
Grilled Steak Nachos	80
Grilled Pork Chops With Bacon Mushroom Sauce	82
Herb-Garlic Crusted Flank Steak With Pan-Roasted Grapes	83
Rosemary Skillet Pork Chops With Quick Braised Cabbage	84
Cornbread And Beef Skillet Pie	85
Beef And Stout Skillet Pie	86
Skillet Shepherd's Pie	89
Buffalo Chicken & Potato Skillet	90
Italian Sausage & Tortellini Skillet	92
Flank Steak Fajitas	93
Perfect Porterhouse Steak	94

Barbecued Deer Meat	95
Chicken Fried Pork With Milk Gravy	96
Sunday Steak With French Butter	97
Seafood	100
Shrimp Fajitas	100
Salt-Roasted Shrimp With Lemon-Honey Dipping Sauce	101
Skillet Shrimp Fajitas Easy Dinner Recipe	102
Fire Roasted Trout	103
Pan-Roasted Sea Bass With Garlic Butter	104
Creamy Salmon Piccata	105
Shrimp Fajitas	107
Cheesy Ravioli Skillet	108
Skillet Shrimp Tacos	109
Skillet Shrimp, Sausage, And Rice	110
Pan-Fried Brook Trout	111
Skillet Fried Rainbow, Brown Or Brook Trout	112
Trout Almondine	113
Brook Or Rainbow Trout Supreme	114
Vegan Meals	115
Three Cheese Mac And Cheese	115
Cabbage Casserole	117
Sweet And Tandy Glazed Carrots With Cranberries	118
Sweet Potato Soufflé	119

Chicken, Apple, Sweet Potato, And Brussels Sprouts Skillet 120

Seared Sausage With Cabbage And Pink Lady Apples 121

Easy Unstuffed Bell Pepper Skillet 122

Sloppy Joe Tater Tot Casserole Recipe 124

20-Minute Skillet Tuscan Tortellini 125

Skillet Scalloped Potatoes 126

Schmaltz-Refried Pinto Beans 127

Poultry 128

Chicken Fajitas 128

La Paix Herb Farm's Rosemary Chicken 129

Simmered Tuscan Chicken 130

Part 1

Recipe 1: Tasty Chicken Enchilada Skillet

This is a great tasting skillet dish to enjoy when you want an easy dish to prepare for the entire family. Easy to make and incredibly delicious, I know you are going to want to enjoy this meal over and over again.

Yield: 6 to 8 Servings

Cooking Time: 15 Minutes

List of Ingredients:

- 12 Tortillas, Corn Variety and Cut Into Small Pieces
- 3 Cups of Chicken, Fully Cooked and Shredded
- 1, 10 Ounce Can of Tomatoes, Finely Diced
- 1, 10 Ounce Can of Enchilada Sauce, Red in Color
- 1, 8 Ounce Can of Tomato Sauce
- ½ Cup of Cheddar, Finely Grated
- ½ Cup of Monterey Jack, Finely Grated
- ½ Of An Avocado, Thinly Sliced

- ¼ Cup of Cilantro, Fresh and Roughly Chopped

Instructions:

1. The first thing that you will want to do is grease a large sized skillet with a generous amount of cooking spray and place over medium heat to heat up.

2. Once hot enough add in your cut up corn tortillas and chicken to your pan. Cook until completed heated through, making sure to stir as often as possible.

3. Pour in your remaining ingredients except for half of your cheese, avocado and cilantro. Stir to thoroughly combine.

4. Cover and cook for the next 5 minutes until piping hot and bubbly.

5. Remove from heat and top with your remaining ingredients. Serve while still piping hot.

Recipe 2: Sour Cream Style Cornbread

This makes for a tasty side dish or as an ingredient to use in a separate dish. This cornbread dish is both moist and completely delicious, I know you will fall in love with it after one bite.

Yield: 8 Servings

Cooking Time: 37 Minutes

List of Ingredients:

- 1 ½ Cup of Cornmeal Mix, White in Color and Self-Rising Variety
- ½ Cup of Flour, All Purpose Variety
- 1 Can of Corn, Cream Style and Low in Sodium
- 1 Container of Sour Cream, Light
- 3 Eggs, Large in Size and Beaten
- 2 Tablespoons of Cilantro, Fresh and Roughly Chopped
- ½ Cup of Cheddar Cheese, Finely Shredded and Reduced in Fat

Instructions:

1. First preheat your oven to 450 degrees. While your oven is heating up use a large sized cast iron skillet and heat in your oven for about 5 minutes.

2. While your skillet is heating up stir together your first 2 ingredients into a large sized bowl. Then add in your next 4 ingredients, stirring thoroughly until evenly blended.

3. Pour this batter into your cast iron skillet, making sure that it is thoroughly greased beforehand.

4. Place into your oven to bake for the next 22 to 25 minutes until they are golden brown in color. Remove from oven and serve right away. Enjoy!

Recipe 3: Easy Sunday Skillet Breakfast

This is an easy breakfast recipe to make for any Sunday morning. It is incredibly hearty and will kick start your Sunday the way it deserves. Feel free to add in some of your favorite veggies and toppings to make this a dish you won't soon forget.

Yield: 6 Servings

Cooking Time: 20 Minutes

List of Ingredients:

- 3 Potatoes, Peeled and Finely Shredded
- 1 tablespoon of Butter, Soft
- 2 Tablespoons of Oil, Vegetable Variety
- 1 Bell Pepper, Red in Color and Finely Diced
- 1 Onion, Medium in Size and Finely Diced
- 1 Clove of Garlic, Minced
- ¾ teaspoons of Salt, For Taste and Evenly Divided
- 6 Eggs, Large in Size and Beaten

- ¼ teaspoons of Pepper, For Taste

Instructions:

1. The first thing that you will want to do is preheat your oven to 350 degrees.

2. While your oven is heating up, place your finely shredded potatoes into a large sized bowl and add in some water enough to cover them. Allow your potatoes to stand for at least 5 minutes before draining and patting dry with a paper towel.

3. Next melt your butter into a medium sized cast iron skillet placed over medium heat. Once your butter is melted, add in your diced pepper and onions, stirring frequently as it cooks for the next 5 minutes.

4. After this time add in your minced garlic and continue to cook for another minute.

5. Add in your potatoes with your salt and continue to cook for the next 10 minutes or until your potatoes are golden in color and tender to the touch. Once done, remove from heat.

6. Make 6 small indentation in your potato mixture and break one egg into each indent. Season your eggs with some salt and pepper.

7. Place your cast iron skillet into your oven and bake for the next 12 to 14 minutes or until your eggs are fully set. Remove and set while still piping hot.

Recipe 4: Pork Chops In Pepper And Jelly Sauce

If you are looking for a tasty and sweet tasting pork recipe, then this is the perfect recipe for you. The jelly sauce that you will use in this recipe will give your pork chops a sweet taste as well as a beautiful glaze that you won't be able to resist.

Yield: 4 Pork Chops

Cooking Time: 33 Minutes

List of Ingredients:

- 4 Pork Chops, Bone in Variety
- 1 teaspoon of Salt
- ¾ teaspoons of Black Pepper, Ground
- 3 Tablespoons of Butter, Soft and Evenly Divided
- 3 Tablespoons of Olive Oil, Extra Virgin Variety
- 1 tablespoon of Flour, All Purpose Variety
- 1 Jalapeno Pepper, Large in Size, Seeded and Finely Minced
- 1/3 Cup of White Wine, Dry Variety

- 1 Cup of Chicken Broth, Homemade Preferable
- ½ Cup of Jelly, Red Pepper Variety

Instructions:

1. The first thing that you will want to do is season your pork chops with a dash of your salt and pepper. Once seasoned add in your butter to your cast iron skillet and set over medium to high heat.

2. Once your skillet is hot enough add in your seasoned pork chops and cook for the next 8 minutes. Then flip and continue cooking for an additional 10 more minutes. After this time remove from heat and set aside.

3. Next add in your all-purpose flour and minced jalapeno to your skillet. Stir to combine and continue cooking for an additional 1 to 2 minutes or until your flour turns golden brown in color. Once brown add in your white wine and use a spatula to loosen up any remaining particles from the bottom of your skillet. Continue cooking for another minute.

4. Then add in your homemade chicken broth and continue cooking until your mixture begins to thicken. This should take at least 2 to 3 more minutes.

5. Last whisk in your jelly until your mixture is smooth in consistency. Continue to cook for another 3 to 4 minutes or until your mixture is thick in consistency. Remove your mixture from heat.

6. Add in your remaining butter and season with some more salt and pepper. Return your pork chops back to your skillet and toss to coat. Serve with your sauce and enjoy!

Recipe 5: Easy Scalloped Potatoes

This dish makes the perfect side dish to accompany your delicious steak or chicken entrée. These potatoes are packed full of delicious Gruyere cheese and this dish will melt in your mouth with every bite that you take.

Yield: 6 Servings

Cooking Time: 1 Hour and 30 Minutes

List of Ingredients:

- 6 Potatoes, Yukon Variety, Peeled and Thinly Sliced
- 3 Tablespoons of Butter, Unsalted and Soft
- 3 Tablespoons of Flour, All Purpose Variety
- 1 ½ Cups of Milk, Whole
- 2 Cups of Cheese, Gruyere Variety and Finely Shredded
- 2 Cloves of Garlic, Minced
- 1 Sprig of Thyme, Fresh
- Dash of Salt and Pepper for Taste

Instructions:

1. The first thing that you will want to do is preheat your oven to 400 degrees.

2. Then heat a medium to large sized skillet over medium heat until hot. Add in your butter and reduce the heat. Add in your flour and whisk vigorously for the next 30 minutes.

3. Then add in your minced garlic, dash of salt and pepper, milk and fresh thyme. Stir to thoroughly combine. Remove from skillet and set aside.

4. Next arrange your potatoes into your skillet, making sure to overlap them. Season each layer you lay out with some salt and pepper and top with your cheese.

5. Pour your milk mixture over your potatoes and top off with your remaining shredded cheese.

6. Cover with some aluminum foil and place into your oven to bake for the next hour. After this time remove your aluminum foil and continue to bake for the next 5 to 10 minutes or until the top of your dish is golden in color.

7. Remove and allow to cool for the next 10 minutes. Serve while still hot and enjoy.

Recipe 6: Wild Rice And Chicken Casserole

This is an easy one pot recipe that the entire family will fall in love with. Mixed with the perfect combination of gravy, ham, mushrooms, rice, making this a wholesome and hearty dish that will leave you feeling full and satisfied for the rest of the day.

Yield: 4 Servings

Cooking Time: 1 Hour and 40 Minutes

List of Ingredients:

- 1 ¼ teaspoons of Salt, Evenly Divided
- 1 Container of Rice, Wild Variety and Uncooked
- 3 Tablespoons of Butter, Soft and Melted
- 1/3 Cup of Flour, All Purpose Variety
- 1 Cup of Milk, Whole
- 2 ½ Cups of Chicken Broth, Homemade Variety
- 1 ½ teaspoons of Mustard, Dry
- ¾ teaspoons of Black Pepper, Ground and Evenly Divided

- ½ Cup of Ham, Country Style and Finely Chopped
- 2 Tablespoons of Olive Oil, Extra Virgin Variety
- 1 Cup of Onions, Yellow in Color and Finely Chopped
- 1 Carrot, Large in Size and Finely Diced
- 8 Ounces of Mushrooms, Fresh and Finely Diced
- 3 Cloves of Garlic, Finely Diced
- 2 Tablespoons of Wine, White in Color
- 4 Chicken Breasts, Skinned and Boned
- Some Parsley, Flat Leaf Variety and For Garnish
- Some Almonds, Finely Sliced and For Garnish

Instructions:

1. The first thing that you will want to do is cook your rice. To do this combine your first two ingredients together in a small sized saucepan and bring to a boil. Once boiling reduce your heat to medium and cover. Cook for the next 30 minutes.

2. While your rice is cooking melt your butter in a large sized saucepan over low heat. Once melted add in your flour, making to whisk thoroughly until smooth. Add in your next 3 ingredients and increase the heat to medium, making sure to whisk constantly. Cook for at least 5 minutes or until your mixture is thick in consistency. Season with a dash of salt and pepper.

3. Next cook your ham in some oil in a large sized cast iron skillet over medium to high heat, making sure to stir occasionally for the next 6 minutes. Cook until your ham begins to brown

thoroughly. Then add in your next 3 ingredients, stirring thoroughly to combine and continue to cook for the next 8 minutes or until your onions are tender to the touch.

4. Add in your garlic and continue to cook for an additional minute. Add in your white wine and cook until it is fully evaporated. Remove from heat.

5. Next preheat your oven to 375 degrees. While your oven is heating up season your chicken with your remaining salt and pepper. Add your remaining oil into a large sized skillet and add in your chicken once it is hot enough. Cook for at least 5 minutes on each side or until your chicken is thoroughly browned. Once cooked remove from heat and transfer onto a plate.

6. Then drain your rice and mix together with your ham and sauce mixture in your cast iron skillet. Place your cooked chicken on top of this mixture.

7. Place into your oven to bake for the next 30 minutes or until your mixture begins to bubble and your chicken is fully cooked. Remove from oven and allow to cool for at least 10 minutes before serving.

Recipe 7: Pecan Fried Catfish

If you are looking for a southern style home cooked meal, then you can't go wrong with this delicious recipe. This dish combines all of the southern style flavors that you won't be able to resist with a hint of a creative twist to it.

Yield: 6 Servings

Cooking Time: 1 Hour and 33 Minutes

List of Ingredients:

- 2 Pounds of Catfish, Cut into Fillet and Cut Into Thin Strips
- 1 Cup of Buttermilk, Warmed
- 1 Cup of Pecans, Finely Ground
- 2/3 Cup of Cornmeal, Plain and Yellow in Color
- 2/3 Cup of Parmesan Cheese, Finely Grated
- 1 tablespoon of Cajun Seasoning
- 1 tablespoon of Paprika
- 2 Eggs, Large in Size and Beaten
- Some Oil, Vegetable Variety

Instructions:

1. The first thing that you will want to do is place your first two ingredients into a large sized Zip lock bag. Seal and shake to combine. Place into your fridge to chill for at least one hour. After this time remove your catfish and toss away your buttermilk.

2. Then add in your oil to your cast iron skillet and heat over medium heat.

3. Next combine your next 5 ingredients together in a medium sized shallow cowl. Then beat your eggs in a separate small sized bowl.

4. Dip your catfish fillets into your beaten eggs and then dredge in your ground pecan mixture, making sure to shake off the extra bits.

5. Place your coated catfish fillets into your hot oil inside of your cast iron skillet. Fry in small batches for the next 2 to 3 minutes or until your fillets are golden brown in color. Once done remove and drain on a plate lined with paper towels. Serve once drained and enjoy.

Recipe 8: Kale And Potato Frittata

This is a great tasting frittata dish that I know you are going to certainly enjoy. You can make this regardless of what time of the day it is, as it makes a great dish regardless.

Yield: 4 Servings

Cooking Time: 30 Minutes

List of Ingredients:

- 6 Eggs, Large in Size and Beaten
- 1 Cup of Half and Half, your Favorite Brand
- 1 teaspoon of Salt, For Taste
- ½ teaspoons of Pepper, For Taste
- 2 Cups of Sweet Potatoes, Finely Diced
- 2 Tablespoons of Olive Oil, Extra Virgin Variety
- 2 Cups of Kale, Packed and Finely Chopped
- ½ Of A Small Onion, Red in Color and Finely Diced

- 2 Cloves of Garlic, Minced
- 3 Ounces of Cheese, Goat Variety

Instructions:

1. First preheat your oven to 350 degrees.

2. While your oven is heating up whisk together your first 4 ingredients in a large sized bowl until thoroughly beaten together.

3. Then use a large sized skillet placed over medium heat. Add in your oil and once it is hot enough add in your diced sweet potatoes and cook for the next 10 minutes or until your potatoes are tender and golden in color. Remove from your skillet and set aside.

4. Then add in your kale and next 2 ingredients into your skillet and cook for the next 5 minutes or until your kale is wilted and tender.

5. Pour your egg mixture over the veggies and continue to cook for the next 4 minutes.

6. Top with your goat cheese and cooked sweet potatoes.

7. Place into your oven to bake for the next 10 to 15 minutes or until your dish is completely set. Remove from your oven and serve.

Recipe 9: Hearty Sweet Potato Salad

This is a great tasting salad that you can enjoy on the coldest of days. With the perfect combination of tasty roasted veggies and savory ginger vinaigrette, I know this is one salad recipe that you are going to want to make over and over again.

Yield: 4 Servings

Cooking Time: 1 Hour and 10 Minutes

List of Ingredients:

- 1 Pound of Sweet Potatoes, Peeled and Cut into Small Wedges
- 1 Onion, Sweet Variety and Cut into Small Wedges
- 1 tablespoon of Olive Oil, Extra Virgin Variety
- 1 Clove of Garlic, Minced
- ¾ teaspoons of Salt, For Taste
- ½ teaspoons of Pepper, Ground
- 1 Pack of Mache, Fresh and Washed

Instructions:

1. The first thing that you will want to do is preheat your oven to 400 degrees.

2. While your oven is heating up, place your cast iron skillet into it and heat up for the next 10 minutes.

3. While your skillet is heating up toss together your first 6 ingredients in a large sized bowl until thoroughly mixed together. Then pour this mixture into your cast iron skillet.

4. Place into your oven to bake for the next 25 minutes, making sure to stir at least once after this time. Continue to bake for the next 15 minutes or until your potatoes become tender.

5. Remove from oven and pour your mixture over your Mache. Serve right away and enjoy.

Recipe 10: Cast Iron Skillet Style Salsa

If you are looking to enjoy a taste of Mexican cuisine, there is no better way to do so then with this tasty dish. This salsa dish is packed full of smoky flavor, I know you won't be able to resist it.

Yield: 1 ½ Cups of Salsa

Cooking Time: 30 Minutes

List of Ingredients:

- 3 Tomatoes, Plum Variety and Cut Into Halves
- 3 Cloves of Garlic, Unpeeled
- 1 Jalapeno Pepper, Green in Color and Cut Into Halves
- 1 Onion, Medium in Size and Cut Into Small Wedges
- 1 ½ Tablespoons of Lime Juice, Fresh
- ¾ teaspoons of Salt, For Taste
- 1/3 Cup of Cilantro Leaves, Fresh and Roughly Chopped

Instructions:

1. The first thing that you will want to do is heat up a large sized skillet over medium heat for the next 5 minutes.

2. Once your skillet is hot enough add in your tomatoes with the cut side down. Add in your next 2 ingredients and cook for the next 6 minutes, making sure to stir once in a while until your tomatoes are slightly charred.

3. Transfer this mixture into a food processor and process on the highest setting until smooth in consistency.

4. Then peel your garlic and add into your food processor. Process again until smooth in consistency.

5. Next add your onion wedges to your cast iron skillet and cook for the next 6 minutes or until slightly charred. Add this to your food processor.

6. Process your mixture for at least 40 seconds until smooth in consistency.

7. Then add in your remaining ingredients and process until smooth in consistency. Pour into a serving bowl and serve right away. Enjoy!

Recipe 11: Fruit Packed Pancakes

This is one recipe that you don't have to worry about preparing extra dishes to go along with it. This dish is packed full of sweet tasting fruit, making it the perfect way to kick off your day.

Yield: 4 Servings

Cooking Time: 35 Minutes

List of Ingredients:

- 4 Eggs, Large in Size and Beaten
- 1 Cup of Milk, Whole
- 1 Cup of Flour, All Purpose Variety
- ¼ teaspoons of Salt, For Taste
- 1/3 Cup of Butter, Melted
- 3 Tablespoons of Marmalade, Orange Flavored
- 3 Tablespoons of Butter, Soft
- 1 tablespoon of Lemon Juice, Fresh

- 1 Pack of Peaches, Frozen and Thawed
- 1 Cup of Blueberries, Frozen and Thawed

Instructions:

1. The first thing that you will want to do is place your cast iron skillet into an oven and bake it at 425 degrees for the next 5 minutes.

2. While your skillet is heating up, combine your first 5 ingredients into a medium sized bowl, whisking thoroughly until evenly combined.

3. Then remove your skillet from your oven and pour your batter into it.

4. Return back to your oven and bake for the next 20 to 25 minutes.

5. While your batter is baking, combine your last ingredients together in a medium sized saucepan and bring your mixture to a boil, making sure to stir your mixture constantly and cook for the next 5 minutes.

6. Remove your skillet from your oven and place your mixture on top of your pancake. Top off with your blueberries and serve right away.

Recipe 12: Sweet Potato Onion Cakes

These tasty little snacks make for the perfect appetizer dish that you will fall in love with after your first bite. Serve these treats with a generous dollop of sour cream for the tastiest results.

Yield: 6 to 8 Servings

Cooking Time: 1 Hour and 5 Minutes

List of Ingredients:

- 4 Sweet Potatoes, Medium in Size
- 2 Eggs, Large in Size and Beaten
- ½ Cup of Flour, All Purpose Variety
- 2 Jalapeno Peppers, Red in Color and Finely Chopped
- 1 ½ teaspoons of Salt, For Taste
- ½ Cup of Green Onions, Thinly Sliced and Evenly Divided
- ¼ Cup of Oil, Canola Variety
- Some Lime Wedges, Fresh and For Garnish

Instructions:

1. Place your sweet potatoes into your microwave and cover with some damp paper towels. Microwave on the highest setting for the next 10 minutes or until the potatoes are tender to the touch. Leave to stand in your microwave for at least 5 minutes.

2. After this time peel your potato and place into a medium sized bowl. Mash half of your potato thoroughly with a fork and grate the other half finely. Mix together both of these types of potatoes.

3. Next add in your next 5 ingredients until thoroughly combined.

4. Then add in your oil to a large sized skillet and heat over medium heat. Drop your mixture into your hot skillet by the tablespoon and cook for the next 6 minutes or until golden brown on both sides. Place on a plate lined with paper towels to drain.

5. Serve with a garnish of green onions and lime wedges and enjoy.

Recipe 13: Succulent Filet Mignon

If you haven't had the chance to try filet mignon, you have to give this recipe a try for yourself. Once you get a taste of it, I can guarantee that you will want to make it over and over again. Serve this with a side of mashed potatoes or a healthy salad to make a great tasting meal.

Yield: 4 Servings

Cooking Time: 20 Minutes

List of Ingredients:

- 4 Beef Fillets, Tenderloin Variety
- 1 teaspoon of Pepper, Fresh
- ½ teaspoons of Salt, For Taste
- 2 Tablespoons of Butter, Soft
- 2 Tablespoons of Olive Oil, Extra Virgin Variety

Instructions:

1. The first thing that you will want to do is season your filet mignons with a dash of salt and pepper.

2. Then melt your soft butter in a large sized cast iron skillet placed over medium heat.

3. Once your skillet is hot enough add in your filet mignons and cook on both sides for the next 5 to 8 minutes or until your fillets are done to your liking.

4. Remove from heat and allow to stand for at least 5 minutes before serving. Enjoy!

Recipe 14: Smoked Trout With Apple Hash

Regardless if you make this tasty dish over a campfire or in the comfort of your own home, this is one dinner dish that I know you are going to want to make over and over again. I recommend serving this dish with a healthy side salad to make a wholesome meal that you won't forget any time soon.

Yield: 4 Servings

Cooking Time: 55 Minutes

List of Ingredients:

- 1 Cup of Sour Cream
- 2 Tablespoons of Horseradish, Prepared Beforehand
- 4 Tablespoons of Butter, Soft
- 2 Russet Potatoes, Unpeeled, Boiled and Diced Finely
- 1 Onion, Yellow in Color, Small in Size and Finely Chopped
- 1 Apple, Granny Smith Variety, Finely Diced
- Dash of Salt For Taste

- Dash of Pepper For Taste
- ½ Cup of Cream, Heavy Variety
- 1 Fillet of Trout, Smoked and Flaked
- 1 ½ teaspoons of Dill, Fresh
- 1 teaspoon of Cloves and Sliced Fresh
- Some Lemon Wedges, For Garnish

Instructions:

1. The first thing that you will want to do is use a large sized cast iron skillet and heat it over medium to high heat for the next 5 minutes.

2. While your skillet is heating up whisk together your first 2 ingredients and place into your fridge to chill until you are ready to use it.

3. Once your skillet is hot, melt your butter and add in your potatoes. Cook your potatoes for about 10 minutes or until they are brown and crispy. Then add in your apples and onion and continue to cook for the next 10 minutes or until your apples are gold in color and your onions are tender to the touch. Season with a dash of salt and pepper for taste.

4. Add in your pepper and your heavy cream. Cook without stirring it for the next 5 minutes or until your potatoes turn a dark gold in color.

5. Then flip your hash gently and continue to cook for the next 5 minutes.

6. Add in your smoked trout and remaining ingredients except for your lemon wedges. Remove from heat.

7. Serve with your lemon wedges for garnish and enjoy alongside your sour cream mixture.

Recipe 15: Cornbread Style Focaccia

This is an Italian style inspired dish that everybody will fall in love with. While this is inspired by tasty Italian cuisine, this dish has a Southern taste to it that you won't be able to resist.

Yield: 8 to 10 Servings

Cooking Time: 40 Minutes

List of Ingredients:

- 2 Cups of Cornmeal Mix, Self-Rising Variety and White in Color
- 2 Cups of Buttermilk
- ½ Cup of Flour, All Purpose Variety
- 1 Package of Yeast, Quick Rising Variety
- 2 Eggs, Large in Size and Beaten
- ¼ Cup of Butter, Soft and Melted
- 2 Tablespoons of Sugar, White
- 1 Cup of Feta Cheese, Crumbled

- 1 Cup of Black Olive, Chopped Coarsely
- ¾ Cup of Tomatoes, Grape Variety and Cut in Half
- 1 tablespoon of Rosemary, Fresh and Chopped Coarsely

Instructions:

1. The first thing that you will want to do is preheat your oven to 375 degrees.

2. While your oven is heating up grease a large sized cast iron skillet and place in your oven to heat for the next 5 minutes.

3. Then mix together your first 7 ingredients together until your mixture is moistened. Pour this mixture into your warm skillet.

4. Top with your remaining ingredients.

5. Place into your oven to bake for the next 30 minutes or until your dish is golden brown in color. Remove from your oven and allow to cool slightly before serving.

Recipe 16: Charred Peppers With Dipping Sauce

If you are looking for a tasty appetizer dish to serve that will surely impress your guests, then this is the perfect dish for you. It is extremely color and will leave your guests craving for more.

Yield: 4 Servings

Cooking Time: 25 Minutes

List of Ingredients:

- ¼ Cup of Feta Cheese, Crumbled
- ¼ Cup of Yogurt, Plain and Greek Variety
- 1 Green Onion, Minced
- 2 teaspoons of Mint, Fresh and Roughly Chopped
- 2 Tablespoons of Lemon Juice, Fresh
- 2 Tablespoons of Olive Oil, Extra Virgin Variety
- Dash of Salt For Taste
- Dash of Pepper For Taste
- 1 Pack of Pepper, Sweet Variety, Mini and Assorted

- 1 tablespoon of Olive Oil, Extra Virgin Variety
- 2 Tablespoons of Lemon Juice, Fresh

Instructions:

1. The first thing that you will want to do is heat up a large sized cast iron skillet over medium to high heat for the next 5 minutes.

2. While your cast iron skillet is heating up, whisk together your first 6 ingredients in a large sized bowl until thoroughly combined. Season with a dash of salt and pepper and all to stand until you are ready to use it.

3. Use a medium sized bowl and toss together your remaining ingredients together. Place this mixture into your hot cast iron skillet, making sure to stir it occasional for the next 8 minutes or until charred and wilted. Remove from heat and transfer to a serving plate.

4. Serve with your feta dip and enjoy.

Recipe 17: Hearty Fried Tomatoes

If you have never tried fried green tomatoes before, you need to try this dish out for yourself. These tomatoes are incredibly juicy on the inside yet salty and hearty on the outside. I promise you, you will love this dish.

Yield: 8 Servings

Cooking Time: 25 Minutes

List of Ingredients:

- 4 Green Tomatoes, Large in Size and Thinly Sliced
- 2 teaspoons of Salt
- 1 teaspoon of Pepper
- Some Cooking Spray
- 1 ½ Cups of Buttermilk
- 2 Cups of Breadcrumbs, Japanese Style
- 1 tablespoon of Creole Seasoning
- 1 teaspoon of Paprika
- 1 Cup of Flour, All Purpose Variety

Instructions:

1. The first thing that you will want to do is preheat your oven to 400 degrees.

2. While your oven is heating up season your green tomatoes with a dash of salt and pepper on both sides.

3. Next take out a large sized baking sheet and line in with some parchment paper. Then grease a wire rack with a generous amount of cooking spray and place on top of your parchment paper and baking sheet.

4. Then pour your buttermilk into a small sized bowl while adding your breadcrumbs and paprika in another small sized bowl.

5. First dredge your tomatoes in your flour, then dip into your buttermilk and last dredge in your breadcrumbs. Spray each coated tomato slice with some cooking spray and place onto your wire rack.

6. Place your tomatoes into your oven to bake for the next 18 to 20 minutes or until golden brown in color, making sure to turn once halfway during the cooking process. Remove from oven and serve right away.

Recipe 18: Blistered Brussel Sprouts

If you have never found the best way to cook up your Brussels sprouts, then you need to try this recipe out for yourself. This dish makes Brussels sprouts that are crispy on the outside yet incredibly tender on the inside. Trust me. This dish is absolutely is delicious.

Yield: 4 Servings

Cooking Time: 15 Minutes

List of Ingredients:

- 1 Pound of Brussels Sprouts, Fresh
- 3 Tablespoons of Oil, Canola Variety
- ¾ teaspoons of Salt, For Taste
- 1 tablespoon of Honey, Pure
- 1 tablespoon of Water, Hot
- 1 tablespoon of Garlic, Minced
- 1 tablespoon of Soy Sauce, Your Favorite Kind
- ¼ teaspoons of red Pepper, Dried and Crushed
- ½ Cup of Mint Leaves, Fresh and Roughly Torn

Instructions:

1. The first thing that you will want to do is heat up a large sized cast iron skillet by placing it over medium to high heat. Heat for the next 5 minutes.

2. Then add in your oil to your cast iron skillet and evenly coat the bottom by swiveling your pan around.

3. Once your oil is hot enough add in your Brussels sprouts in a single layer. Cook for the next 5 minutes or until golden brown in color. Season with a dash of salt and continue to cook for another 2 minutes.

4. While your Brussels sprouts are cooking, whisk together your honey and hot water together.

5. Add in your remaining ingredients except for your fresh mint leaves in to your Brussels sprouts. Add in your honey mixture and stir to thoroughly combine.

6. Remove from heat and stir in your fresh mint leaves. Serve immediately and enjoy.

Recipe 19: Pork Style Quesadillas

Your cast iron skillet is one of the best tools to use for a variety dishes and this is one of them. With this tasty dish you can make incredibly cheesy quesadillas that can make a great tasting appetizer or main dish for the entire family to enjoy.

Yield: 4 to 6 Servings

Cooking Time: 12 Minutes

List of Ingredients:

- ½ Pound of Pork, Shredded and Barbecued Flavored
- ½ Cup of Barbecue Sauce, Your Favorite Kind
- ¼ Cup of Cilantro, Fresh and Roughly Chopped
- 5 Onions, Green in Color and Minced
- 8 Tortillas, Floured Variety
- 1 Cup of Mexican Style Cheese, Four Cheese Variety and Finely Shredded
- 2 Tablespoons of Butter, Soft and Melted

- Some Sour Cream, For Toppings
- Some Green Onions, Finely Sliced, For Toppings
- Some Barbecue Sauce, For Toppings
- Some Cilantro, Fresh, Roughly Chopped and For Toppings

Instructions:

1. First stir together your first 4 ingredients together in a large sized bowl until thoroughly mixed together.

2. Spoon some of your mixture into the center of your tortillas and top off with some shredded cheese.

3. Next fold your tortillas in half, making sure to press firmly to seal. Then spread your soft butter over both sides of your tortillas.

4. Then heat up a large sized cast iron skillet over medium heat and cook up your tortillas for the next 2 to 3 minutes on both sides or until thoroughly browned in color.

5. Remove from heat and cut in half. Serve with your desired toppings and enjoy.

Recipe 20: Braised Turnips

While turnips may seem far from appetizing, I just know you are going to enjoy this particular recipe. They are healthy to enjoy and taste surprisingly delicious. I know you won't be able to get enough of it after your first bite.

Yield: 4 Servings

Cooking Time: 35 Minutes

List of Ingredients:

- 15 Turnips, Small in Size and White in Color
- 2 Tablespoons of Butter, Soft
- 3 Tablespoons of Vinegar, Apple Cider Variety
- Dash of Salt, For Taste
- 2 Tablespoons of Honey, Pure
- 1 tablespoon of Butter, Soft

Instructions:

1. The first thing that you will need to do is heat up a large sized cast iron skillet over medium to high heat for at least 5 minutes.

2. While your cast iron skillet is heating up trim your turnips and cut them in half.

3. Then melt your butter in your hot cast iron skillet and add in your turnips in a single layer and cook without touching them for at least 5 minutes or until they are golden brown in color.

4. Next pour your vinegar over your golden brown turnips. Then add in some water until your turnips are at least ¼ inch deep. Season with a dash of salt.

5. Bring this mixture to a boil before reducing the heat to low or medium. Allow your mixture to simmer for at least 5 minutes or until your turnips are crispy and tender to the touch.

6. Once crispy increase your heat to medium and bring to a boil while uncovered. Allow your turnips to boil for the next 5 minutes or until your liquid has almost completely evaporated.

7. Continue to cook, making sure to turn once in a while for the next 10 minutes or until all of your liquid has evaporated.

8. Then stir in your honey and remaining butter and remove from heat. Serve while still piping hot and enjoy.

Recipe 21: Sweet Tasting Apricot Cinnamon Rolls

This is a great tasting and warm breakfast snack that you will certainly enjoy. Feel free to substitute in your raisins, fruits or chocolate chips to this recipe if you wish. Remember, it is for you so make it accordingly to your taste.

Yield: 12 Rolls

Cooking Time: 90 Minutes

List of Ingredients:

- 1 Pack of Biscuits, Frozen
- 1 Pack of Apricots, Dried
- Some Flour, All Purpose Variety
- ¼ Cup of Butter, Soft and Melted
- ¾ Cup of Brown Sugar, Firm and Packed
- 1 teaspoon of Cinnamon, Ground

- ½ Cup of Pecans, Toasted and Finely Chopped
- 1 Cup of Sugar, Powdered Variety
- 3 Tablespoons of Milk, Whole
- ½ teaspoons of Vanilla, Pure

Instructions:

1. The first thing that you will want to do is arrange your biscuits nicely onto a surface that is slightly floured. Make sure that your biscuits are not touching. Let your biscuits stand for at least 35 to 45 minutes or until your biscuits are completely thawed.

2. While your biscuits are sitting out, pour some boiling water over your apricots. Allow your apricots to stand for at least 10 minutes before finely chopping them.

3. Next sprinkle your biscuits with some flour and press the edges together. Form your dough into a rectangle and spread your soft butter over the surface of it. Then top your dough with your apricots, pecans, brown sugar and ground cinnamon.

4. Roll up your biscuits and cut into 12 thick slices. Place your cut rolls into a large sized cast iron skillet.

5. Place into an oven preheated to 375 for the next 35 to 45 minutes or until your rolls are golden brown in color. Remove from your oven and allow to cool.

6. While your rolls are baking, take out a small sized bowl and stir together your powdered sugar, vanilla and milk until thoroughly combined and smooth in consistency. Pour this mixture over your rolls and serve while still warm. Enjoy!

Recipe 22: Apple And Cinnamon "Pancake"

This is a dish that resembled a soufflé of sorts and is just as delicious. Once you family gets a taste of it, I guarantee that they will be begging you for the recipe. I recommend using fat free or low fat milk with this recipe to make it puffier.

Yield: 6 Servings

Cooking Time: 45 Minutes

List of Ingredients:

- 1 Apple, Gala Variety, Peeled and Thinly Sliced
- 1 tablespoon of Sugar, White
- 3 Tablespoons of Butter, Soft and Evenly Divided
- 2 Eggs, Large in Size and Beaten
- ½ Cup of Milk, Fat Free or Low in Fat
- ½ Cup of Flour, All Purpose Variety
- ½ teaspoons of Cinnamon, Ground
- ¼ teaspoons of Salt, For Taste

- ¼ teaspoons of Nutmeg, Ground
- 1 Cup of Sour Cream
- ½ Cup of Brown Sugar, Light and Packed
- 2 Tablespoons of Apple Cider, Fresh
- Some Powdered Sugar, For Garnish

Instructions:

1. The first thing that you will want to do is preheat your oven to 450 degrees.

2. While your oven is heating up, heat up a large sized cast iron skillet over medium to high heat for the next 5 minutes.

3. Next add in your first 2 ingredients into a small sized bowl and toss thoroughly to combine.

4. Then melt your butter in your hot cast iron skillet. Once melted add in your apples and cook for the next 5 minutes or until tender to the touch. Remove from your cast iron skillet and make sure your skillet is wiped clean.

5. Next whisk together your eggs and chosen milk in a medium sized bowl. Once thoroughly beaten add in your next 4 ingredients and whish thoroughly to combine.

6. Melt your remaining butter into your cleaned cast iron skillet over medium to high heat. Once melted add in your egg mixture and top off with your fully cooked apples.

7. Place this into your oven to bake for the next 20 minutes or until your pancake is golden in color and puffy.

8. While your pancake is baking stir together your light brown sugar and sour cream together and heat in your microwave for the next 45 seconds. After this time whisk thoroughly until your sugar is fully dissolved.

9. Stir in your apple cider and stir to thoroughly combine. Serve with your hot pancake and garnish with your powdered sugar. Enjoy while still warm.

Recipe 23: Pecan Fried Okra

Fried Okra make for a delicious and healthy snack that you won't be able to get enough of. This is a great tasting Southern style dish that you can serve as an appetizer or a main course.

Yield: 6 to 8 Servings

Cooking Time: 22 Minutes

List of Ingredients:

- 1 Cup of Pecans, Finely Chopped
- 1 ½ Cups of Baking Mix, All Purpose Variety
- 1 teaspoon of Salt, For Taste
- ½ teaspoons of Pepper, For Taste
- 2 Packs of Okra, Whole, Frozen and Thawed
- Some Peanut Oil

Instructions:

1. First place your finely chopped pecans into a large sized shallow baking dish. Place this dish into your oven to bake for the next 10 minutes at 350 degrees or until toasted lightly.

2. After this time remove your pecans from the oven and place into a food process along with your next 3 ingredients and process on high until finely ground in texture. Next place this mixture into a large sized bowl.

3. Add in your okra and toss thoroughly to coat. Press your toasted pecan mixture into your okra mixture.

4. Add your oil to a large sized cast iron skillet and heat over high heat until piping hot. Add in your coated okra and fry for the next 5 to 6 minutes or until golden in color. After this time remove and drain on a plate lined with paper towels. Serve once slightly cooled.

Recipe 24: Wholesome Top Shelf Baked Chicken

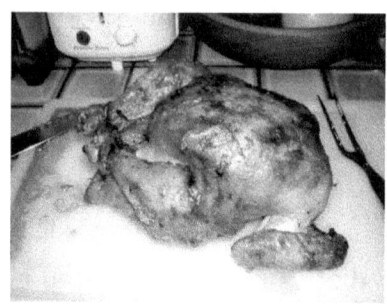

If you have never heard of top shelf chicken, you need to try this recipe out for yourself. This dish makes chicken that is extremely crispy on the outside while packed full of flavor and juice on the inside. I highly recommend serving this dish with some baked red potatoes to make a truly delicious meal that you will never forget.

Yield: 4 Servings

Cooking Time: 1 Hour and 50 Minutes

List of Ingredients:

- 1 Pound of Red Potatoes, Cut Into Halves
- 3 teaspoons of Salt, For Taste and evenly Divided
- 3 to 4 Pounds of Chicken, Whole
- 2 Tablespoons of Olive Oil, Extra Virgin Variety and Evenly Divided
- ½ teaspoons of Black Pepper, For Taste

- 12 Sprigs of Rosemary, Fresh
- 2 Lemons, Fresh and Cut Into Halves

Instructions:

1. The first thing that you will want to do is bring your halved red potatoes, dash of salt and a generous amount of water to a boil is a large sized saucepan over high heat. Once the water begins to boil reduce the heat to medium and allow your potatoes to simmer for at least 10 minutes or until they are tender to the touch.

2. Next seat up your oven to 350 degrees. While your oven is heating up prepare your chicken by ensuring that the neck and giblets are removed. Cut your chicken alongside the backbone and discarding it. Tuck the wing tips under your chicken and season with a dash of salt and pepper.

3. Then heat up a large sized cast iron skillet over medium heat for the next 10 minutes. Add in some oil to your skillet and once it is hot enough add in your red potatoes, making sure that the cut side is faced downward.

4. Place your chicken on top of your potatoes and top off with your sprigs of rosemary. Place into your oven to bake for the next 15 minutes or until your chicken is brown in color. Remove and place your chicken onto a grill. Place your skillet on top of it and grill for the next 45 minutes or until your chicken has an internal temperature of 165 degrees. Remove and allow to cool for at least 5 minutes.

5. Next add your lemons onto your grill and bake for at least 5 minutes or until they are slightly charred. Serve with your chicken and potatoes and enjoy.

Recipe 25: Upside Down Pineapple And Carrot Cake

With one simple flip of this tasty cake and you will have a moist cake on your hand. The caramelized fruit adds a delicious twist to this dessert dish that you won't be able to resist.

Yield: 8 Servings

Cooking Time: 1 Hour and 15 Minutes

List of Ingredients:

- ¼ Cup of Butter, Soft and Melted
- 1 Can of Pineapple, Slices in Juice and Fully Drained
- 7 Cherries, Maraschino Variety and Without Stems
- 1 Cup of Sugar, White
- ½ Cup of Vegetable Oil
- 2 Eggs, Large in Size and Beaten
- 1 Cup of Flour, All Purpose Variety
- 1 teaspoon of Baker's Style Baking Powder

- 1 teaspoon of Cinnamon, Ground
- ¾ Cup of Baker's Style Baking Soda
- ½ teaspoons of Salt
- 1 ½ Cups of Carrots, Fresh and Finely Grated
- ½ Cup of Pecans, Finely Chopped

Instructions:

1. The first thing that you will want to do is preheat your oven to 350 degrees.

2. While your oven is heating up melt your butter in a large sized cast iron skillet over low heat. Then add in your brown sugar and pineapple slices in a single layer, making sure to reserve your pineapple juice. Place at least 1 cherry in the center of every pineapple slice.

3. Next beat together your next 3 ingredients in a small sized bowl with an electric mixer until thoroughly beaten.

4. Then use a separate medium sized bowl and mix together your next 5 ingredients until evenly mixed. Add this to your sugar mixture and beat with your electric mixture until evenly blended.

5. Stir in your remaining ingredients and mix until thoroughly mixed. Spoon this batter over your pineapple slices.

6. Place into your oven to bake for the next 45 to 50 minutes or until thoroughly set. Remove from oven and transfer to a wire rack to cool for the next 10 minutes.

7. Once cooled slip your cake onto a plate and serve right away.

Part 2

Breakfast

Carrot-Zucchini-Nut Muffins

Ingredients:

- 1/2 cup of chopped pecans
- 1/2 tsp salt
- 1 tsp ground cinnamon
- 1 medium zucchini, shredded
- 2 eggs, beaten
- 3/4 cup orange juice
- 1/4 cup butter, melted
- 1/2 cup sugar
- 1 cup whole wheat flour
- 1/2 tsp baking soda
- 1 tsp vanilla
- 1 tsp baking powder
- 1 cup all purpose flour
- 2 medium carrots, shredded

Instructions:

- Preheat oven to 400 degrees. Combine first 7 dry ingredients in a large bowl. In another bowl, stir together egg, orange juice, butter and vanilla; add to dry ingredients, stirring just until moistened. Fold in carrots, zucchini and pecans.

- Spoon into greased muffin pans, filling 2/3 full. Bake for 20 minutes. Remove from pans immediately and cool on wire racks. Very good topped with a cream cheese frosting.

Mountain Man Breakfast

Ingredients:

- 2 pounds sausage
- 2 pounds frozen hash brown potatoes
- 8 eggs, beaten with ¼ cup water
- 2 cups cheese, grated

Instructions:

- Fry and crumble sausage.
- Using the sausage drippings in the pan, brown potatoes and spread them evenly in bottom of oven.
- Place cooked sausage over potatoes.
- Pour eggs over sausage layer. Sprinkle top with cheese.

Johnna's Ham And Cheese Cornbread

Ingredients:

- ½ cup cheddar cheese, shredded
- 1½ cups biscuit mix
- 1 cup ham, small cubes

- 1¾ cups milk
- 2 tablespoons sugar
- 1½ teaspoons baking powder
- 2 eggs, lightly beaten
- 1 teaspoon salt
- ¼ cup oil
- 1½ cups white cornmeal

Instructions:

- Make a mixture of cornmeal, baking powder, biscuit mix, sugar and salt in a bowl. Add eggs, cubed ham milk and cheese.
- Heat half of oil in cast iron pan; add other half of oil to the mixture.
- Pour batter into the pan. Bake at 450°F for 25 minutes.

Full Count Cornbread

Ingredients:

- 1 teaspoon salt
- 2/3 cup white sugar, optional
- 3 medium eggs
- 2 cup butter
- ½ teaspoon baking soda
- 2 cups buttermilk

- 2 cups white flour, unbleached
- 3 cups yellow cornmeal, whole kernel
- 6 teaspoons baking powder

Instructions:

- Preheat oven to 375°F. Mix ingredients in a bowl.
- Heat iron pan in an oven and melt butter in it while preparing other ingredients.
- Mix most of the butter into dry ingredients except a generous butter coating in the pan.
- Add eggs and buttermilk, mixing well until a thick, smooth batter is formed. (*Slightly more than 2 cups of buttermilk may be needed.)
- Pour cornbread batter into warm cast iron pan; place in oven.
- Check after 30 minutes of baking. An additional 15 minutes or so of baking time may be required.
- If so, move iron pan to another location in oven to ensure even baking.
- Cornbread is finished baking when it is browned and risen and may split open.
- Remove from oven, cut; butter for immediate enjoyment!

Upside Down Salsa Cornbread

Ingredients:

- 2 cups Teays Valley® Cornbread Mix
- 1 cup shredded cheddar cheese
- 1 tablespoon sugar
- salsa, medium hot
- 4 tablespoons vegetable oil
- 1 teaspoon salt
- 1 medium bell pepper, seeded, cut in rings
- ½ teaspoon garlic salt
- 1 pound ground beef chuck
- 1 16-ounce jar Fire Creek®
- 1¼ cups milk1 egg
- 1 medium onion, chopped
- 1 teaspoon chili powder

Instructions:

- Cook the chuck along with onions and spices until the chuck is no longer red.
- Move mixture to one side; place half of pepper rings.
- Repeat this procedure. Spread ground chuck mixture over pepper rings.

- Mix sugar combine cornmeal mix, salsa, cheese milk, egg and vegetable oil.
- Preheat oven 425°F over 40 minutes. Place the mixture in the oven. Turn upside down on serving dish.

Skillet Cornbread

Ingredients:

- 2 teaspoons butter
- 3 teaspoons sugar
- 1 teaspoon baking soda
- 2 cups milk
- a teaspoon salt
- 2 eggs
- 1 a cups yellow cornmeal cup flour, all-purpose
- 1 cup buttermilk

Instructions:

- Preheat oven to 400°F. Put and heat butter in cast iron pan. Cook cornmeal, soda, flour, sugar and salt together.
- Stir in milk, eggs and buttermilk.
- Pour into pan. Pour 1 cup milk over corn mixture. Don't stir.
- Bake for 35 minutes.
- Cut and serve.

Mexican Cornbread

Ingredients:

- 1 cup self-rising cornmeal
- 3 tablespoons sugar
- 1 cup self-rising flour
- 1 green bell pepper, chopped
- ¾ cup onions, chopped
- 1 cup milk
- 1 8-ounce can creamed corn
- 1 egg
- ¾ cup vegetable oil
- 1 banana pepper, chopped
- ½ cup hot cheese or longhorn cheese, shredded

Instructions:

- Mix all ingredients and pour in a skillet pan.
- Bake at 350°F about 1 hour.

Fall Run Jalapeno Cornbread

Ingredients:

- 1 cup all-purpose flour, sifted
- 1 tablespoon sugar
- 1 cup yellow or white cornmeal

- ¾ teaspoon salt
- 1 cup milk
- 1 jalapeno red pepper, seeded and chopped fine
- 2 tablespoons melted shortening or oil
- 4 teaspoons baking powder
- 1 egg, beaten

Instructions:

- Mix well flour, cornmeal, sugar, baking powder and salt in bowl.
- Add milk, egg, and jalapenos. Stir.
- Pour in cast iron and bake at 450° F for 15-20 minutes.

Peach Upside Down Cake

Ingredients:

- 1 stick butter
- 1½ cups sugar
- 2 eggs
- 2 teaspoons baking powder
- 2 cups flour
- 1 teaspoon salt
- 1 cup milk
- 1 teaspoon vanilla

Instructions:

- Mix Cream butter, eggs, sugar, and salt altogether.
- Make a flour mixture with milk with baking soda. Add vanilla
- Put a layer of brown sugar on pan.
- Place peach halves on the pan.
- Pour batter over the pan and bake.
- Any kind of fruit can be used.

Pineapple Upside Down Cake

Ingredients:

- ½ stick butter
- 1 can pineapple slices
- 1 cup brown sugar
- 1 yellow cake mix – prepared
- 4 maraschino cherries, halved

Instructions:

- Melt butter in pan. Smooth brown sugar in the pan. Place pineapple rings to cover the pan
- Place cherry in middle of pineapple rings.
- Pour cake batter over the top. Bake until done.

Cornbread

Ingredients:

- 1½ cups yellow cornmeal

- 1 tablespoon baking powder
- 1 teaspoon sugar
- 1 egg
- ½ teaspoon baking soda
- 1 teaspoon salt
- ¼ cup cooking oil
- 1 cup buttermilk
- ½ cup flour

Instructions:

- Mix in a large bowl egg, buttermilk, baking soda, flour and salt.
- Mix cornmeal, sugar, baking powder and oil.
- Grease cast iron.
- Pour batter.
- Bake until done.

Grandma Charlotte's Black Magic Corn Bread

Ingredients:

- 1 tablespoon bacon fat
- ¾ cup white flour
- 1¼ cups cornmeal, stone ground
- 2 teaspoons baking powder
- 2 tablespoons shortening, melted

- 1½ cups buttermilk
- ½ teaspoon baking soda
- 1 tablespoon sugar
- 1 egg

Instructions:

- Preheat oven to 450°F. Heat the pan.
- Mix all ingredients.
- Pour batter into hot cast iron pan.
- Bake until done.
- Serve.

Fancy West Virginia Cornbread

Ingredients:

- ½ teaspoon salt
- 1 15-ounce can creamed style corn, drained
- 1 8-ounce sour cream
- ½ cup vegetable oil
- 2 cups cornmeal, self-rising
- 3 eggs, beaten
- 1 tablespoon sugar

Instructions:

- Mix ingredients together.
- Grease pan and pour mixture into the pan.

- Bake until golden brown.

My Crusty Cornbread

Ingredients:

- 1½ cups flour, self-rising
- 1½ tablespoons sugar
- 1 cup cornmeal, self-rising
- 1 egg (optional)
- 2 tablespoons margarine or oil
- 1½ cups sweet milk

Instructions:

- Mix all ingredients.
- Pour mixture cast iron.
- Bake 35-40 minutes.

Wv Skillet Upside Down Cake

Ingredients:

- ½ stick margarine
- 1 20-ounce can pineapple slices (reserve juice)
- 1 cup brown sugar
- ¾ cup sugar
- 1½ teaspoons salt
- 1¼ cups plain flour

- 1 egg
- 2 teaspoons vanilla
- 2 teaspoons baking powder
- ½ cup pineapple juice

Instructions:

- Melt margarine in skillet.
- Sprinkle brown sugar over margarine.
- Place pineapple slices.
- Mix ingredients and pour on skillet.
- Bake 25-30 minutes until golden brown.

Raspberry Skillet Cake

Ingredients:

- 1 cups all-purpose flour
- ½ teaspoon baking soda
- 1½ teaspoons baking powder
- 4 tablespoons butter or margarine, room temperature, divided a cup light brown sugar
- 1 cup granulated sugar
- 1 teaspoon orange zest, grated
- ½ teaspoon salt
- 2 cups red raspberries
- 2 egg whites

- b cup orange juice

Instructions:

- Preheat oven to 350°F.
- Combine flour, baking soda and salt. In skillet, melt 1 tbsp. butter over low heat. Remove from heat. Stir in brown sugar.
- Spread berries over sugar. Mix butter and casting sugar.
- Mix eggs and zest until creamy.
- Spread batter over berries.
- Bake 45-50 minutes.

Spiced Pear Skillet Cake

Ingredients:

- 1 cup light brown sugar, firmly packed
- 1a cups flour, all-purpose
- 6 tablespoons unsalted butter, cut into 4 pieces (¾ stick)
- 2 teaspoons ground cinnamon
- ½ teaspoons salt
- ½ cup corn oil or vegetable oil
- 1 tablespoon ginger, fresh, grated, peeled
- 4 medium pears, peeled, cored, each cut into 6 wedges (about 1.5 pounds)
- 1a cups granulated sugar
- 1¼ teaspoons baking soda

- 2 eggs
- 1 small pear, unpeeled, coarsely grated
- 2 scoops vanilla ice cream (optional)

Instructions:

- Preheat oven to 350°.
- Sprinkle brown sugar evenly over bottom of skillet.
- Melt butter on skillet.
- Mix flour, sugar, cinnamon, baking soda and salt in bowl.
- Using electric mixer, beat in eggs and oil. Mix in grated pear and ginger.
- Arrange pears on skillet and pour batter over pears.
- Bake.

Meat (Beef, Pork, Lamb)

Beef Fajitas

Ingredients:

- 2 pounds sirloin beef steaks, cut into strips
- 1 tablespoon cumin
- 3 tablespoons cooking oil
- 3 tomatoes, cut into wedges
- 2 tablespoons chili powder
- 1 large red pepper, cut into strip
- 1 large green pepper, cut into strip
- 2 medium onions, cut into strips
- 1 large yellow pepper, cut into strip
- 1 16-ounce package flour tortillas

Instructions:

- In cast iron brown beef strips in oil. Sprinkle with spices.
- Sauté peppers and onion strips. Add spices, meat and tomatoes.

Iron Skillet Ramps And Bacon

Ingredients:

- ½ pound bacon, chunked or finely minced

- 1 pound fresh ramps or leeks, cleaned
- 1 tablespoon oil

Instructions:

- Put bacon in skillet with oil and fry until done.
- Place ramps in skillet with bacon.
- Cook until done.

Spiced Pork Tenderloin With Sautéed Apples

Ingredients:

- 1/8 teaspoon ground cinnamon 1/8 teaspoon ground nutmeg
- 1 pound pork tenderloin, trimmed and cut crosswise into 12 pieces Cooking spray
- 2 tablespoons butter
- 3/8 teaspoon salt
- 2 cups thinly sliced unpeeled Braeburn or Gala apple
- 1/3 cup thinly sliced shallots 1/8 teaspoon salt
- 1/4 teaspoon freshly ground black pepper
- 1/4 cup apple cider
- 1/4 teaspoon ground coriander
- 1 teaspoon fresh thyme leaves

Instructions:

- Heat a large cast-iron skillet over medium-high heat. Combine first five ingredients; sprinkle spice mixture evenly over pork.
- Coat pan with cooking spray. Add pork to pan; cook three minutes on each side or until it is done as desired.
- Remove pork from pan; keep warm. 2. Melt butter in pan; swirl to coat.
- Add apple slices, 1/3 cup shallots, and 1/8 teaspoon salt; sauté 4 minutes or until apple starts to brown. Add apple cider to pan, and cook for 2 minutes or until apple is crisp-tender.
- Stir in thyme leaves. Serve apple mixture with the pork.

Easy Beef Stew

Ingredients:

- 2 tbsp. Oil
- 1 package of McCormick Beef Stew Seasoning Mix
- 2 (14.5 oz) cans of diced tomatoes in sauce
- 1 package of frozen gumbo vegetable mix
- 5 medium russet potatoes peeled and diced
- 2 cups water
- 3 tbsp. flour

Instructions:

- Coat beef with flour. Heat oil in large deep cast iron skillet on medium heat
- Add beef; cook until beef is brown on all sides. Stir it in seasoning mix and water. Simmer for about 45 minutes or until beef is tender.
- Add potatoes, tomatoes and vegetable mix and simmer until vegetables are tender stirring occasionally.

Coalminer's Pie

Ingredients:

- 1 cup chopped onions
- 15 ounce can tomato soup
- 1 lb. Ground Beef
- 1 tsp pepper
- 1 teaspoon chili powder
- 2 medium bell peppers
- 1 tsp flour
- 1 cup corn meal
- 1 1/2 tsp salt
- 2 eggs
- 1 can corn, drained
- 1 tsp shortening oil
- 1/2 cup milk

Instructions:

- Preheat oven to 350 degrees. Brown meat and onion, stir in tomato sauce, bell pepper, corn, chili powder, 1 tsp salt and pepper.
- Bring to a boil, lower heat.
- Cover and simmer for 15 minutes. Pour into 10.25 inch cast iron skillet. Beat together eggs, oil and milk for 1 minute in a small bowl.
- Beat in cornmeal, flour and salt until well blended. Pour over meat to cover entire surface.
- Bake for 20 minutes.

Bacon And Pimento Cheese Pizza

Ingredients:

Crust

- 2 cups King Author Unbleached All-Purpose Flour
- ½ teaspoon active dry yeast
- ¾ teaspoon salt
- 1 tablespoon olive oil, plus 1½ tablespoons for the pan
- ¾ cup warm water

Toppings

- 6 ounces mozzarella, grated (about 1 ¼ cups, loosely packed)
- ½ cup pimento cheese

- ½ cup pizza sauce
- ½ cup crumbled bacon

Pimento Cheese
- 1 cup shredded sharp cheddar cheese
- ¼ teaspoon garlic powder
- ¼ cup mayonnaise (we love Duke's mayo in the south)
- 1 roasted jalapeno, seeded and diced
- salt and pepper
- 3 tablespoons diced pimentos

Instructions:
- Mix flour, salt, yeast, water, and 1 tablespoon olive oil in a bowl to make dough.
- Gather dough into a ball.
- Prepare your skillet 3 hours before you want to serve your pizza. Pour 1½ tablespoons olive oil.
- Place dough in pan.
- Cover and let rise for 2 hours at room temperature.

Pimento Cheese:
- Combine cheese, mayonnaise, garlic powder, jalapeno, and pimentos. Mix well.
- Season with salt and pepper to taste.

Kenny's Country Gravy

Ingredients:
- ¼ cup rough-chopped yellow onion
- 4 tablespoons bacon fat

- 2 tablespoons fresh sage
- ¼ teaspoon black peppercorns
- ¼ Benton's ham hock
- 1 cup milk
- ground black pepper
- ¼ cup all-purpose flour
- ¼ teaspoon crushed red pepper
- 1 cup heavy cream
- kosher salt

Instructions:

- Sweat the yellow onion, ham hock, sage, black pepper, and crushed red pepper until the onion is translucent in a pan.
- Add cream and milk. Let it rest for 30 minutes.
- In a cast iron make a roux by melting the remaining bacon fat and whisking in the flour until smooth. Put milk mixture into the roux.
- Serve and enjoy.

Skillet S'mores Dip

Ingredients:

- 1 tablespoon butter
- 10 ounces large marshmallows
- 24 ounces semi-sweet chocolate morsels
- Graham crackers.

Instructions:

- Preheat oven.

- Place a skillet inside the preheated oven for 5 minutes.
- Remove skillet from oven. Melt butter in the skillet, covering the cooking surface evenly.
- Pour chocolate morsels and top with marshmallows.
- Bake for 7-10 minutes, until marshmallows are toasted.

Thick Cut Salt & Pepper Pork Chops

Ingredients:

- 2 boneless pork chops
- 2 tablespoons peanut oil
- Salt and peppers.

Instructions:

- Preheat oven.
- Brush pork chops with peanut oil.
- Gradually preheat cast iron pan.
- Sear pork chops.
- Remove from stovetop and bake for 4-6 minutes.

Grilled Steak Nachos

Ingredients

Steak

- 1 skirt steak, flank steak or flap steak
- Salt and pepper, to taste
- 1 lime, juiced

Nachos

- 1 bag tortilla chips
- 1 16 ounce can corn, washed
- 1 15 ounce can black beans, washed
- 2.5 cups Monterey Jack cheese
- 1 lime, juiced
- Dollop of sour cream
- 4.5 ounce can green chiles, washed
- ½ cup fresh cilantro, chopped
- Salt and pepper, to taste.

Instructions:

- Season the outside of your steak with lime juice, salt, and pepper.
- Preheat grill-side. Cook steaks.
- While steaks are cooking, layer the inside of the cast iron with tortilla chips, then add black beans, corn, green chiles, and cheese. Repeat these layers 2-3 times.
- Once the steaks are done, pull them off the grill and let them rest, 10 minutes.
- Take the hot grill lid off the fire and put the nacho-filled wok on the stand.
- Add the hot lid on top to cover the nachos and melt the cheese.
- Cook.
- Slice steak and add to nachos along with lime juice, cilantro, and sour cream.

Grilled Pork Chops With Bacon Mushroom Sauce

Ingredients

- 3-4 bone-in pork chops
- 2 tablespoons freshly cracked black pepper
- 2 tablespoons dijon mustard
- 1.5 tablespoons dried oregano
- 4 slices of bacon, dried
- ¼ cup white wine
- 1.5 cups baby bella mushrooms, sliced
- 1.5 tablespoons garlic powder
- 1 tablespoon fine sea salt
- ¼ cup shallots, chopped
- 1 ¼ cups spinach
- 1 tablespoon lemon juice.

Instructions:

- Create a medium size fire to fit the Cook-It-All. Separate into the wok and the skillet. When fire begins to start breaking down into coals, add Cook-It-All to preheat for 2-3 minutes.
- Lather pork chops with dijon mustard and season with black pepper, garlic powder, dried oregano and sea salt. Add chops to skillet and let cook for 8 minutes per side.
- While chops are cooking, add bacon to wok and cook for about 5 minutes per side.

- When chops are halfway done, add mushrooms and shallots to wok and cook for 2 minutes.
- Finally, add a white wine & spinach to wok and let simmer for another 5 minutes.
- Stir occasionally and finish with lemon juice on top.
- Once chops are done, add mushroom sauce on top of meat and enjoy!

Herb-Garlic Crusted Flank Steak With Pan-Roasted Grapes

Ingredients

- 2 tsp. fresh thyme
- 2 tsp. fresh rosemary
- 1 large garlic clove
- 1 1/2 tsp. Kosher salt
- 3/4 tsp. Freshly ground pepper
- 1 flank steak
- 2 tbsp. olive oil
- 3 c. assorted whole grapes
- 2 shallots
- 2 tbsp. white balsamic vinegar
- 1/2 c. freshly crumbled blue cheese

Instructions:

- Combine first 5 ingredients. Rub steak with herb mixture. Heat 1 tablespoon oil in a large, heavy skillet over medium-high heat. Cook steak 6 to 7 minutes on each side or until desired degree of doneness. Remove and cover loosely with foil.
- Reduce heat to medium. Add remaining 1 tablespoon of oil to pan, and sauté grapes and shallots 5 to 6 minutes or until grapes just begin to soften.
- Remove from heat, and let stand 1 minute. Stir in vinegar and season with salt and pepper to taste.
- Slice steak against the grain into thin slices. Arrange on a serving platter, spooning grapes and cheese over meat. Sprinkle with additional fresh herbs if desired. Serve with mashed potatoes.

Rosemary Skillet Pork Chops With Quick Braised Cabbage

Ingredients

- 3 tbsp. olive oil
- 4 small bone-in pork chops
- Kosher salt
- pepper
- 8 small Garlic cloves
- 4 sprig fresh rosemary
- 1 red onion

- 1 small head red cabbage
- 2 tsp. sugar
- 4 tbsp. balsamic vinegar

Instructions:

- Heat oven to 425 degrees F. Heat 2 tablespoons oil in a large oven-safe skillet over medium-high heat. Season the pork chops with 1/2 teaspoon each salt and pepper and cook on one side until golden brown, 3 to 4 minutes.
- Turn the chops, scatter the garlic and rosemary around the chops and cook for 2 minutes more. Transfer the skillet to the oven and roast until the chops are just cooked through, 6 to 8 minutes. Let the chops rest for 5 minutes before serving.
- Meanwhile, heat the remaining tablespoon oil in a second large skillet over medium heat. Add the onion and 1/2 teaspoon each salt and pepper and cook, covered, stirring occasionally, for 5 minutes.
- Add the cabbage, sugar, 2 tablespoons vinegar and 3 tablespoons water and simmer, covered, until nearly all the liquid has evaporated and the cabbage is just tender, 10 to 12 minutes; stir in the remaining vinegar. Serve with the pork chops, garlic and rosemary.

Cornbread And Beef Skillet Pie

Ingredients

- 1 lb. Lean Ground Beef

- 1 can Ranchero Beans
- 1 can corn kernels
- 1 package cornbread mix (plus the required ingredients to make it)
- 2 oz. pepperjack cheese

Instructions:

- Heat oven to 400 degrees F. In a large oven-safe skillet, cook beef over medium-high heat, breaking it up with the back of a spoon until browned, 5 to 7 minutes. Stir in the beans and corn and cook simmer for 2 minutes.
- Meanwhile, prepare the cornbread according to package directions. Spread the cornbread batter over the beef mixture, leaving a 1/2-inch border all the way around. Sprinkle with cheese.
- Bake until golden brown and a toothpick inserted into the cornbread comes out clean, 15 to 20 minutes. Let cool for 5 minutes before serving.

Beef And Stout Skillet Pie

Ingredients

- 1 tbsp. olive oil
- 1 lb. Lean Ground Beef
- 4 oz. small shiitake mushrooms
- Kosher salt

- pepper
- 2 tbsp. tomato paste
- 1/2 c. frozen pearl onions
- 1 tbsp. fresh thyme leaves
- 3 tbsp. all-purpose flour
- 8 oz. stout (we used Guinness)
- 2 c. frozen butternut squash pieces
- 1 c. frozen peas
- 1 refrigerated rolled pie crust
- 1 large Egg

Instructions:

- Heat oven to 375 degrees F. Heat the oil in a 9-inch cast-iron skillet over medium heat. Add the beef, mushrooms and 3/4 teaspoon each salt and pepper, and cook, breaking up the beef with a spoon, until browned, 4 to 6 minutes. Spoon off and discard any fat.
- Add the tomato paste and cook, stirring, for 2 minutes. Stir in the onions and thyme, then sprinkle with the flour and cook, stirring, for 30 seconds.
- Add the stout and simmer until the liquid has thickened, about 1 minute. Add 1/2 cup water and bring to a simmer. Add the squash and peas, return to a simmer, then remove from heat. (This whole step takes only 2 to 3 minutes total.)
- Unroll the pastry on a cutting board, brush with the egg, then cut a cross in the center. Lay the dough on top of the

beef mixture (egg-side up), gently pressing the edges around the inside of the skillet. Bake until golden brown, 30 to 35 minutes. Let rest for 5 minutes before serving.

Skillet Shepherd's Pie

Ingredients

For Meat Mixture

- 1 tbsp olive oil
- 1 1/4 lb ground beef lean
- 1/2 tsp salt or to taste
- 1/2 tsp pepper or to taste
- 1 large onion chopped
- 1 clove garlic minced
- 1/2 tsp red pepper flakes
- 2 tbsp Worcestershire sauce
- 1.9 oz onion soup mix I used Knorr, 55g pkg
- 1 cup beef broth low sodium
- 2 cups frozen veggies I used mix of peas, carrots, green beans and corn

For Mashed Potatoes

- 6 large potatoes peeled and cut into cubes
- 4 tbsp butter softened
- 2/3 cup milk
- 1/4 cup Parmesan cheese
- 1/2 tsp salt or to taste
- 1/2 tsp white pepper or to taste
- 1 tbsp parsley fresh, for garnish

Instructions

- **Boil the potatoes:** Start by first cooking the potatoes in boiling water for about 15 minutes or until fork tender.

While the potatoes are cooking, you can prepare the meat mixture.

- **Prepare the meat mixture:** Heat the oil in a large skillet over medium heat. Add the ground beef to the skillet, season it with the salt and pepper and cook it for about 5 minutes or until it's no longer pink, breaking it up as you go along.
- Add the onion and garlic and cook for 3 more minutes until the onion softens and becomes translucent. Add the pepper flakes, Worcestershire sauce, onion soup mix, beef broth and stir. Stir in the frozen veggies and cook for a couple more minutes. Set aside.
- Preheat the oven 350 F degrees.
- **Prepare the mashed potatoes:** Drain the potatoes then add them to a large bowl. Add in the butter and using a potato masher, mash until smooth. Add the milk, Parmesan cheese, salt pepper and mash a bit a more until smooth.
- **Finish assembling the shepherd's pie:** Spread the potatoes over the meat and smooth with a spoon. Take a fork and rough up the top a bit and garnish with a bit of parsley.
- **Bake:** Place the skillet on a baking sheet, then place it in the oven and bake for 40 minutes until golden brown on top.
- Garnish with more parsley and pepper and serve warm.

Buffalo Chicken & Potato Skillet

Ingredients

- 2 pounds baby potatoes (the tiniest you can find)
- 1-2 cups reduced-sodium chicken stock or broth

- 3 T unsalted butter
- 1 rotisserie chicken (meat shredded and the rest discarded)
- 1 16- ounce bottle buffalo wing sauce
- 1/2 cup crumbled blue cheese
- 1 celery stalk (diced)
- 1/2 cup ranch dressing (can also use blue cheese dressing or thinned sour cream)

Instructions

- Place one layer of baby potatoes in a 12-inch cast-iron skillet, fitting slightly snugly. Pour chicken stock over potatoes just until halfway up their sides. Bring to a boil over medium-high heat. Reduce heat to medium, cover skillet and cook for 5 minutes.
- Remove the cover from skillet and cook another 5 minutes. Cut butter into three pieces and lay each piece of butter in a different spot over the potatoes, allowing to melt. DO NOT STIR. Keep cooking until all liquid has evaporated and you hear a sizzling sound – that sound means that the potatoes are now starting to brown. Using something flat-bottomed (I use a tamper but anything flat-bottomed will do), gently press down on each potato to flatten gently (it's okay if they split, you want to gently "pop" them). Now just leave them alone to brown – no stirring – for another 5 minutes or so, checking the bottoms occasionally.
- Meanwhile, add enough buffalo wing sauce to thoroughly coat chicken, then gently heat in microwave until just hot (don't heat chicken until coated with sauce or it will become dry).

- Place chicken mixture on top of potatoes in skillet. Top with blue cheese crumbles, diced celery, and drizzle with ranch dressing. Serve immediately.

Italian Sausage & Tortellini Skillet

Ingredients

- 1/2 cup diced onion
- 1 teaspoon minced garlic (2 cloves)
- 1 pound Ground Italian Sausage mild or spicy
- 1 24-ounce jar of your favorite spaghetti sauce or marinara
- 1 20-ounce package of fresh cheese tortellini 2 9-ounce packages will do
- 1/2 cup water
- 1 teaspoon Italian seasoning
- 1 1/2 cups freshly grated Mozzarella cheese
- 1/2 cup freshly shredded Parmesan cheese
- Fresh chopped parsley or basil optional

Instructions

- Heat an oven safe skillet over medium-high heat. Melt 1 tablespoon olive oil and add onions, cooking for a couple of minutes or until they begin to soften.

- Stir in minced garlic and add crumbled italian sausage. Cook until no longer pink. Drain off any extra grease.

- Stir in spaghetti sauce, water, Italian seasoning and Tortellini. Bring to a boil, stirring occasionally, then cover and reduce heat to low. Simmer for about 8 minutes, or until tortellini is tender.

- Remove from heat. Sprinkle Mozzarella can Parmesan cheeses evenly over tortellini. Cover the skillet with the lid and let sit for 5 minutes while the cheeses melt. Alternatively, you could place the skillet under the broiler for a 2-3 minutes or until golden, melted and bubbly.
- Garnish with fresh chopped parsley or basil if desired.

Flank Steak Fajitas

Ingredients

- 2 clove garlic
- 1 lb. beef flank steak
- 1 bunch radishes
- Salt and pepper
- 2 limes
- 1/2 c. reduced-fat sour cream
- 8 fajita-size flour tortillas
- 2 tsp. vegetable oil
- 3 poblano peppers
- 1 medium onion
- 1/4 c. water

Instructions:

- Rub garlic all over steak, and let stand at room temperature. In small colander or sieve, toss radishes with 1/8 teaspoon salt. Place colander over bowl, cover, and refrigerate. Into small bowl, grate peel from 1 lime and cut lime into quarters; set aside. Stir sour cream into lime peel. Cover bowl and refrigerate.

- Preheat toaster oven to 300°F. Wrap tortillas in foil, and heat in toaster oven 15 minutes or until warm and pliable.

- Heat 12-inch cast iron or other heavy skillet on medium-high until hot. Brush garlic off steak and discard. Squeeze juice from lime quarters all over steak, then sprinkle with ¼ teaspoon salt and ¼ teaspoon freshly ground black pepper to season both sides. Add 1 teaspoon oil to skillet, then add steak. Cook 10 minutes for medium-rare, or until desired doneness, turning over once. Transfer steak to cutting board; reduce heat to medium.

- Add remaining 1 teaspoon oil to skillet, and add peppers and onion. Cook 2 to 3 minutes or until onion browns, stirring occasionally. Add 1/4 cup water and cook 5 minutes longer or until vegetables are tender, stirring occasionally.

- Cut steak across the grain into thin slices. Cut remaining lime into wedges. Divide steak and vegetables among tortillas; top with lime sour cream. Serve with radish salad and lime wedges.

Perfect Porterhouse Steak

Ingredients

- 1 2"-thick Porterhouse steak, trimmed (about 2 lb.)
- 1 tablespoon vegetable oil
- Kosher salt and freshly ground black pepper
- 3 tablespoons unsalted butter, room temperature

Instructions:

- Let steak sit at room temperature 30 minutes before cooking, which will help it cook quickly and more evenly.
- Heat broiler. Heat a large skillet, preferably cast iron, over medium-high heat, then heat oil in pan until smoking. Season steak very generously with salt and pepper and cook until a deep brown crust forms on underside (do not turn), about 4 minutes. Transfer steak to a cutting board, turning it browned side up.
- Cut meat from bone in 2 pieces (strip steak and filet mignon). Slice both pieces straight down perpendicular to the bone 1" thick. Replace sliced steak around the bone (it should look like a whole sliced steak) and return to skillet, browned side up. Top with butter and broil until butter is melted and steak is medium-rare, 4–6 minutes. Serve steak with buttery pan juices spooned over.

Barbecued Deer Meat

Ingredients:

- 3 tablespoons vinegar
- 3 teaspoons Worcestershire sauce
- 1 cup onions, chopped

- 1 teaspoon chili powder
- 1 pound deer meat
- 1 15-ounce can tomatoes
- ¾ cup ketchup
- 2 tablespoons shortening
- ½ teaspoon salt

Instructions:

- Melt shortening in iron skillet.
- Add onion and meat; cook until onion is tender and meat is brown.
- Add all other ingredients and cook 20 minutes. Add water if too thick.

Chicken Fried Pork With Milk Gravy

Ingredients:
- 4 rib pork chops, boneless (½" thick) or 1½ pounds
- 1¾ teaspoons salt
- 2 cups vegetable oil
- 3¼ cups whole milk
- 2 cups all-purpose flour
- 1 large egg
- 3 tablespoons all-purpose flour
- 1½ teaspoons black pepper

Instructions:

- Preheat oven to 250°F. Pound pork chops on both sides with rough-textured
  side of meat pounder until ¼" thick.
- Season with salt and pepper; cut into 3 inch pieces.
- Whisk together 2 cups flour, 1 teaspoon salt, and 1 teaspoon pepper in a shallow dish.
- Whisk together egg, ¾ cup milk, remaining ¾ teaspoon salt and ½ teaspoon pepper in another shallow dish.
- Dip pork pieces in egg mixture to coat, then dredge in flour
- Transfer pork as coated to large rack set on a baking sheet.
- Let pork stand, uncovered, at room temperature 15 minutes.
- Heat oil in deep 10" cast iron skillet over high heat until thermometer registers 375°F.
- Fry pork in batches, turning over once, until golden, about 4 minutes per batch, transferring to paper towels to drain. Return oil to 375°F between batches.

Keep pork warm on clean baking sheet in oven. Pour off all but 2 tablespoons oil into a heat proof bowl, leaving any brown bits in bottom of skillet. Add remaining 3 tablespoons flour to skillet; cook roux over moderate heat, stirring constantly, 3 minutes. Bring to a boil; whisk in remaining 2½ cups milk. Reduce heat and simmer, whisking occasionally, until thickened, about 5 minutes. Season gravy with salt and pepper and serve over pork.

Sunday Steak With French Butter

Ingredients

- **2** porterhouse steaks, 1 pound each
- **1 pinch** Kosher salt
- **1** stick unsalted butter
- **1 1/2 tablespoons** flat leaf parsley, chopped
- **1/2 teaspoon** garlic, minced
- **1 teaspoon** shallot, minced
- **1 pinch** Freshly ground white pepper
- **1/2** fresh lemon
- **1 splash** Oil

Instructions:

- At least 6 hours before and up to the day before you plan to cook the steaks place them on a cooling rack set over a tray with edges. You want to catch the drips.
- Season both sides of the steaks with salt. Put them back into the fridge uncovered until an hour before you want to cook them.
- Allow the butter to soften at room temperature. Meanwhile place the garlic, shallot and parsley into a mortar. Using the pestle bruise, crush, and pulverize the aromatics until they are mushy.
- Place the butter into a small mixing bowl and smear it around with a rubber spatula. Add the aromatics, a few drops of lemon juice, a pinch of salt and a few grinds of white pepper. Blend the butter until it is one shade of green with no streaks.

- You can either refrigerate the butter as is or you can roll it up in parchment pepper, then foil and twist the ends to form a round log. The foil allows the ends to stay sealed.
- When your are ready to cook the steaks, season both sides with fresh ground black pepper. Place a cast iron skillet over medium high heat. Add enough oil to coat the bottom of the pan. When the oil is hot -- you don't want it too hot but you want it to start searing right away -- add the steak. Cook the steak on both sides until it is very brown and caramelized. Remove the steak from the pan when it has reached one temperature below where you like. If you want it cooked medium then cook the steak to medium rare and so on. Remove the steak to a sheet tray.
- Cook the second steak in the same fashion. Both steaks can be cooked up to an hour in advance and left to sit at room temperature. Do not refrigerate them.
- In your oven place the top rack so it is about 8 to 10 inches from the broiler. Heat the broiler.
- Using a filet knife cut the meat from each side of the bone then slice the meat into smaller bit size pieces. Re-assemble the steaks on the sheet tray. Smear each steak with some softened maitre d'butter then place a small glob on each steak.
- Place the steaks under the broiler just long enough to melt the butter and heat the steaks through. Serve.

Seafood

Shrimp Fajitas

Ingredients:

- 1 pound medium shrimp
- 1 garlic clove, minced
- 1 cup cilantro, lightly packed
- 4-6 flour tortillas
- 2 large green peppers, stemmed, seeded and thinly sliced
- 1 16-ounce jar WV salsa of choice
- a cup lime juice
- 1 tablespoon cooking oil
- 1 large onion, thinly sliced
- 2 cup plain nonfat yogurt

Instructions:

- Stir together shrimp, cilantro, garlic and lime juice.
- Wrap tortillas in foil; place in skillet.
- Heat oil in cast iron fajita skillet or griddle. Add peppers and onions, stir over medium heat until soften, remove; keep warm.
- Add shrimp to skillet, increase heat to high; cook. Add warm onions and peppers and remaining cilantro, garlic & lime juice mixture to skillet.

- Warm flour tortillas by placing them in heated iron skillet for 5-10 seconds on each side.
- Spoon warm shrimp mixture into tortillas.

Salt-Roasted Shrimp With Lemon-Honey Dipping Sauce

Ingredients:

- One 4-pound box rock salt
- 2 teaspoons grated lemon rind
- 2 tablespoons minced green onions
- 1 garlic clove, minced
- 24 unpeeled jumbo shrimp (about 1 1/2 pounds)
- 2 tablespoons honey
- 1 teaspoon low-sodium soy sauce
- 1/3 cup fresh lemon juice (about 4 lemons)
- 1/8 teaspoon ground red pepper

Instructions:

- Preheat oven to 400°.
- Pour salt in an even layer in a shallow large cast-iron skillet or roasting pan

- Place roasting pan in oven at 400° for 30 minutes or until salt becomes very hot.
- Arrange shrimp in a single layer over salt. Cover with foil and bake at 400° for 5 minutes or until shrimp are done.
- Combine the rind and remaining ingredients; serve sauce with shrimp.

Skillet Shrimp Fajitas Easy Dinner Recipe

Ingredients:

- 1 1/2 pounds of shrimp peeled and deveined, tails removed patted dry
- 1 red bell pepper sliced thin
- 1 yellow bell pepper sliced thin
- 1 small red onion sliced thin
- 1 orange bell pepper sliced thin
- 1 1/2 tablespoons of extra virgin olive oil divided
- 1 teaspoon of kosher salt
- 2 teaspoons of chili powder
- 1/2 teaspoon of onion powder
- 1/2 teaspoon of smoked paprika
- several turns of freshly ground pepper
- 1/2 teaspoon of garlic powder
- 1/2 teaspoon of ground cumin

- Lime
- fresh cilantro for garnish
- tortillas, warmed

Instructions:

- In a small bowl, combine salt, pepper, chili powder, garlic powder, onion powder, cumin and smoked paprika.
- Heat 1 tablespoon of olive oil in iron pan.
- Add onions and bell peppers and cook.
- Push onions and bell peppers to the side of the skillet to make room for the shrimp.
- Add remaining olive oil to skillet, followed by shrimp and remaining seasoning mixture.
- Sauté shrimp until pink and cooked through.

Fire Roasted Trout

Ingredients:

- 2 tablespoons lemon juice
- 1 bunch of dill, chopped
- 2 tablespoons olive oil
- 2 whole trout, butterflied
- 2 lemons, sliced
- salt & pepper

Instructions:

- Set the Cook-It-All's griddle in a bed of coals, smooth side up. Preheat to medium-high heat.

- Combine lemon juice, olive oil and 2 teaspoons chopped dill. Whisk until well incorporated.
- Place remaining dill and lemon slices inside the butterflied trout, brush all over with lemon juice mixture.
- Season with salt and pepper.
- Place fish on preheated griddle and cook each side for 7-10 min. or until the flesh flakes easily. Brush with lemon juice mixture as needed.
- Remove trout from the griddle and serve immediately.

Pan-Roasted Sea Bass With Garlic Butter

Ingredients

Chive Garlic Compound Butter

- 1 cup (2 sticks) unsalted butter, at room temperature
- 1 clove garlic, minced
- 2 tablespoons finely minced fresh chives
- Pinch of kosher salt

Pan-roasted Sea Bass

- 4 sea bass fillets (4-6 ounces each)
- 2 tablespoons olive oil
- Kosher salt and freshly ground black pepper

Instructions:

Chive Garlic Compound Butter:

- In a medium bowl, with an electric mixer, beat the butter until light and fluffy.

- Add the chives, garlic, and salt and mix until thoroughly combined. Spoon the mixture in the shape of a log onto a piece of wax or parchment paper.
- Fold the paper over itself. Using your hands, shape the butter into a cylinder about 1 ½ inches wide (almost like making a Tootsie Roll). Once it is shaped, twist the ends to seal it.
- Place in the freezer to set, about 20 minutes. Refrigerate until ready to serve or up to a month.
- When ready to serve, slice the roll into ¼-inch-thick rounds and remove the parchment. (Only 4 slices of compound butter are need for this recipe.)

Sea Bass:
- Preheat the oven to 375 degrees Fahrenheit.
- Generously season the sea bass with salt and pepper. In a large cast iron skillet over medium heat, warm the oil until a few water droplets sizzle when carefully sprinkled in the skillet. Sear the sea bass, skin side up, until it is well browned and easily releases from pan, about 4 minutes. Flip over and cook until seared, about 1 minute. Transfer the pan to the oven and roast about 5 minutes or cooked to the desired degree of doneness.
- Serve each fillet with a slice of compound butter on top.

Creamy Salmon Piccata

Ingredients
- 4 (6 oz) skinless salmon fillets

- 1 Tbsp olive oil
- Salt and freshly ground black pepper
- 1 Tbsp minced garlic (3 cloves)
- 1 1/4 cups + 1 Tbsp low-sodium chicken broth, divided
- 2 tsp cornstarch
- 1/3 cup heavy cream
- 2 Tbsp fresh lemon juice
- 1 Tbsp butter
- 1 Tbsp minced fresh dill
- 2 Tbsp capers, rinsed
- 1 Tbsp minced fresh parsley

Instructions

- If you have time let salmon rest at room temperature 10 minutes.
- Heat a 12-inch heavy bottomed non-stick skillet over medium-high heat. Add olive oil.
- Dab salmon dry with paper towels. Season both sides lightly with salt and pepper.
- Place in skillet and sear until bottom is golden brown, about 4 minutes. Carefully flip then continue to cook until salmon is cooked through, about 2 - 3 minutes longer.
- Transfer salmon to a plate and cover with foil to keep warm, leave about 1 tsp oil in skillet. Add garlic and saute just until golden brown, about 20 seconds.
- Pour in 1 1/4 cups chicken broth and let simmer until broth is reduced by half, about 4 minutes. Meanwhile in a small bowl whisk together remaining 1 Tbsp broth with cornstarch.
- While whisking pour cornstarch mixture into reduced broth mixture. Cook and stir until thickened, about 1 minute.

- Stir in cream, butter, lemon and dill. Remove from heat, return salmon to skillet.
- Spoon sauce over salmon. Sprinkle with capers and parsley. Serve

Shrimp Fajitas

Ingredients

- 1 tablespoon vegetable oil
- 2 cups sliced bell peppers red, orange, yellow or a combination
- 1 onion thinly sliced
- 2 teaspoons chili powder
- 1/2 teaspoon ground cumin
- 1/4 teaspoon garlic powder
- 1/4 teaspoon onion powder
- 1/2 teaspoon smoked paprika
- 2 tablespoons chopped cilantro
- 1 pound large shrimp peeled and deveined, tails removed if desired
- lime wedges for serving optional
- flour tortillas and fajita toppings of your choice
- salt and pepper to taste

Instructions

- Heat the oil in a large pan over high heat. Add the peppers and onion to the pan and cook, stirring occasionally, until vegetables are tender and charred on the edges. Season the vegetables with salt and pepper.

- In a small bowl, mix together the chili powder, cumin, garlic powder, onion powder, smoked paprika, and salt and pepper to taste.
- Add the shrimp to the pan and sprinkle the seasoning blend over the shrimp and vegetables. Stir to combine.
- Cook for 4-5 minutes or until shrimp are pink and opaque.
- Sprinkle the cilantro over the top and serve. Garnish with lime wedges if desired. Serve the flour tortillas and toppings on the side and have everyone assemble their own fajitas.

Cheesy Ravioli Skillet

Ingredients

- 2 teaspoons olive oil
- 2 cloves garlic minced
- 1 lb. Italian sausage casing removed
- 15 oz BUITONI Marinara Sauce
    - 2 teaspoons **Italian seasoning**
- salt and pepper to taste
- 1 cup low sodium chicken broth or water
- 1 package 18 ounces BUITONI Tomato & Mozzarella Ravioli
- 1/2 cup shredded Italian blend cheese
- 1/4 cup fresh basil chopped

Instructions

- Heat a large skillet over medium/high heat. Add the olive oil and garlic and heat for approximately 3 minutes until fragrant.

- Add in the sausage and cook for 3-5 minutes, crumbling as you cook.
- Stir in the tomato sauce, Italian seasoning, and salt and pepper to taste.
- Add in the broth (or water) and ravioli. Stir to make sure the ravioli is as covered as possible.
- Bring to a boil and then reduce heat to simmer.
- Cook covered for 5 minutes and then uncovered for an additional 5 minutes, or until the ravioli is fully cooked and tender.
- Sprinkle with the shredded cheese. Allow to simmer until cheese is fully melted.
- Sprinkle with the fresh basil.
- Serve and enjoy!

Skillet Shrimp Tacos

Ingredients

- 2 tsp. grated lime zest
- 2 tbsp. freshly squeezed lime juice
- 4 c. thinly sliced red cabbage
- 12 oz. small shrimp
- 1/4 c. fresh cilantro
- 2 tbsp. canola oil
- sour cream
- Hot pepper sauce

- Lime wedges

Instructions:

- In a large bowl, toss cabbage an lime juice.
- In a separate bowl, toss shrimp with cilantro and lime zest.
- In 12-inch skillet, heat canola oil on medium-high until very hot; add shrimp in single layer. Cook another 2 minutes, or until opaque throughout.
- Serve shrimp in flour tortillas with cabbage mixture, sour cream, hot pepper sauce, and lime wedges, if desired.

Skillet Shrimp, Sausage, And Rice

Ingredients

- 2 tbsp. olive oil
- 6 oz. fully cooked andouille sausage
- 1 medium onion
- 1 red pepper
- 2 clove garlic
- 1 c. long-grain white rice
- 1/2 c. dry white wine
- 2 tsp. Creole seasoning
- 1 3/4 c. low-sodium chicken broth
- 12 oz. peeled and deveined shrimp
- 12 oz. plum tomatoes

- 1/2 c. fresh flat-leaf parsley

Instructions:

- Heat the oil in a large skillet over medium-high heat. Add the sausage and cook until browned, 1 to 2 minutes per side; transfer to a plate.
- Reduce the heat to medium, add the onion and cook, covered, stirring occasionally, for 4 minutes. Add the pepper and garlic and cook, stirring occasionally, until the vegetables are just tender, about 5 minutes more.
- Stir in the rice, then the wine and seasoning and bring to a simmer. Add the broth and bring to a boil. Reduce heat and simmer, covered, for 12 minutes.
- Fold the sausage into the rice mixture, then nestle the shrimp in the partially cooked rice and cook, covered, until the shrimp are opaque throughout and the rice is tender, 4 to 5 minutes more. Fold in the tomatoes and sprinkle with the parsley before serving.

Pan-Fried Brook Trout

Ingredients:
- 8 slices bacon
- Salt
- 4 whole brook trout
- Freshly ground black pepper
- 2 cups white or yellow cornmeal

Instructions:

- In large cast iron skillet, cook bacon over medium heat until crisp. Transfer bacon to paper towels to drain.
- Leave bacon fat in the skillet. Dry trout, sprinkle inside and out with salt and pepper; dredge in cornmeal, shaking off excess. Heat bacon fat in skillet. Add trout and cook it for about 5 minutes.
- Turn it on both sides until it is browned from both sides
- Drain on paper towels. Serve trout on platter with bacon used for garnish.

Skillet Fried Rainbow, Brown Or Brook Trout

Ingredients:

- ¾ cup all-purpose flour
- 1 teaspoon salt
- 3 tablespoons vegetable oil
- 2 tablespoons parsley, fresh, chopped
- ¼ cup pecans, chopped
- 1 stick unsalted butter
- 2 whole brook, rainbow, or brown trout
- ¼ teaspoon black pepper
- 1 tablespoon lemon juice, fresh squeezed

Instructions:

- Preheat oven to 200°F. Melt 2 tablespoons butter in 12 inches cast iron skillet over low temperature and remove it from heat
- Rinse trout; pat dry. Brush with melted butter inside and out; season with ¾ teaspoon salt. Dredge each fish in flour to coat completely, shaking off excess.
- Add oil and 2 tablespoons butter to skillet; heat over moderately high heat until foam subsides until foam subsides
- Fry both trout turning over once using spatulas until it is golden for about 8 minutes. Remove trout to sering platter
- Pour off fat from skillet; wipe clean. Melt remaining ½ stick butter over moderate low heat and cook pecans, stirring until fragrant and darker for about 1 to 2 minutes.
- Add lemon juice, stirring to incorporate and spoon over trout. Serve immediately.

Trout Almondine

Ingredients:
- 2 tablespoons butter
- 2 tablespoons lemon juice
- ½ cup all-purpose flour
- 1 egg, beaten
- ¼ cup butter, melted
- 2 tablespoons cooking oil
- 4-6 cleaned trout
- ¼ cup milk
- ¼ cup sliced almonds

Instructions:

- Bone trout. Add salt and pepper to taste.
- Combine egg and milk in bowl. Dredge trout in flour, then in egg mixture and again in the flour.
- In a large skillet, heat oil and 2 tablespoons butter.
- Add trout and fry for 5-6 minutes on each side.
- In skillet, cook almonds in the ¼ cup melted butter until almonds are browned.
- Remove from heat and stir in lemon juice. Place trout on a warm serving platter and pour almonds over and serve immediately

Brook Or Rainbow Trout Supreme

Ingredients:
- ½ teaspoon salt
- 1 egg, beaten
- 1 2-ounce can sliced
- Salt and pepper to taste
- ½ cup butter
- ½ cup bread crumbs
- 2 tablespoons milk
- 1 tablespoon lemon juice
- Lemon juice to taste
- 4 trout, cleaned

Instructions:

- Sprinkle trout inside and out with lemon juice, salt and pepper.
- Combine egg with milk and dip trout in mixture.
- Coat with bread crumbs.
- Melt ¼ cup butter in large cast iron skillet.
- Add fish and fry until golden brown on both sides for about 3 to 4minutes..
- Melt remaining butter in separate skillet. Add mushrooms, 1 tablespoon lemon juice, and ½ teaspoon salt.

Fry until mushrooms are hot. Place trout on serving platter and spoon mushrooms on top.

Vegan Meals

Three Cheese Mac And Cheese

Ingredients:

- 2 tablespoons all-purpose flour
- 1 extra large egg yolk
- 1½ cups heavy cream
- 2 garlic cloves, minced

- 5 ounces goat cheese, shredded
- 3 ounces sharp white cheddar
- 3 tablespoons finely chopped yellow onion
- ½ cup packed freshly grated parmesan
- ¾ pound penne
- 1½ teaspoons chopped fresh thyme Salt and freshly ground pepper
- ¾ teaspoon lemon zest
- 2 tablespoons sour cream

Instructions:
- Heat oven to 400 degree. Butter a 10-inch cast-iron skillet.
- In a pot of boiling salted water, cook pasta until it is firm to bite. Drain and return to pot. Meanwhile, in a large saucepan, onion, bring heavy cream and garlic to a simmer. Transfer ½ cup of the cream to a medium bowl and gradually whisk in flour and return mixture to saucepan.
- Set the bowl aside and continue whisking over moderate heat until thickened, about 3 minutes. Remove from heat and whisk in the goat cheese, cheddar and half of the Parmesan until melted. Stir in the sour cream, zest and 1 teaspoon of thyme and season with salt and pepper.
- Place the egg yolk in the medium bowl and gradually whisk in ½ cup cheese sauce. Gradually whisk the egg mixture into the saucepan.

- Pour cheese sauce over pasta and toss to coat evenly. Add pasta to cast-iron skillet and sprinkle with remaining cheese. Bake for about 25 minutes, until bubbling and golden brown. Sprinkle with remaining thyme.
- Allow mac and cheese to rest for about 5 minutes (if you can stand it), then serve.

Cabbage Casserole

Ingredients:

- 1 cup half and half cream
- 1 small Bell pepper, chopped
- 2 1/2 cups Cheddar cheese, shredded and divided
- Salt and pepper to taste
- 1 clove garlic, minced
- 2 medium onions, chopped
- 1/4 cup unsalted butter
- 1 cup bread crumbs
- 1 large cabbage, chopped, cooked and drained

Instructions:

- Preheat oven to 350 degrees.
- Fry onion, Bell pepper and garlic in butter in deep skillet.
- Add cabbage, 2 cups cheese, bread crumbs, salt and pepper. Mix well.

- Top with 1/2 cup cheese and pour half and half over the top.
- Bake for 30-40 minutes.

Sweet And Tandy Glazed Carrots With Cranberries

Ingredients:

- 1 tbsp. finely chopped fresh flat-leaf parsley
- 1 tbsp. finely chopped fresh flat-leaf parsley
- 1 tbsp. finely chopped fresh flat-leaf parsley
- 2 tbsp. sherry vinegar or white wine vinegar
- 1 tsp salt 1/2 cup good quality chicken stock
- 1 1/2 pounds young carrots, peeled, or large carrots, cut lengthwise into quarters and then in half crosswise
- 1/4 cup dried cranberries
- 1 tbsp. unsalted butter
- 2 tbsp. thyme honey or other variety

Instructions:

- Combine the carrots, oil and salt in a bowl. Heat a cast iron skillet large enough to hold the carrots in a single layer over medium heat just until hot, about 3 ½ minutes. Scrape the carrots into the pan and cook for two minutes, stirring once or twice. Stir in the stock and butter, cover the skillet, and reduce the heat to low, and cook until the carrots are almost tender when pierced with the tip of a knife, about 15 minutes.

- Uncover and stir in the cranberries, honey and vinegar; bring to a boil and cook until the liquid reduced to glaze the carrots, about 5 minutes, shaking the pan occasionally.

- Stir in the parsley and serve.

Sweet Potato Soufflé

Ingredients:

- 3 tablespoons chilled salted butter, cut into small pieces
- 3 tablespoons packed light brown sugar
- ¼ cup apple cider
- 1 teaspoon salt
- 1 teaspoon grated orange zest
- ½ teaspoon ground cinnamon
- 8 medium sweet potatoes or yams (about 4 pounds
- 5 tablespoons salted butter, at room temperature)
- ½ cup half-and-half

Instructions:

- Position a rack in the center of the oven and preheat to 350°F. Put the sweet potatoes in a large stockpot, cover the stockpot with cold water, and then add salt.
- Bring to a boil over high heat. Reduce the heat to medium and cook the potatoes until they are soft when pierced for 30 to 40 minutes. Drain and allow it to cool.
- Peel the sweet potatoes and place in a large bowl. Mash to a coarse consistency with a potato ricer or masher. Add the room-temperature butter, half-and-half, apple cider, brown sugar, cinnamon, and orange zest.
- Beat with an electric mixer on medium speed until it is fluffy for about 2 minutes. Transfer to a buttered 10- or 12-inch cast iron skillet. Dot the potatoes with the chilled butter pieces and bake in the oven until the top is golden brown, about thirty minutes.
- For a perfect golden crust on top, broil for the last five minutes.

Chicken, Apple, Sweet Potato, And Brussels Sprouts Skillet

Ingredients
- 1 tablespoon olive oil
- 1 teaspoon kosher salt — divided
- 1 pound boneless skinless chicken breasts, — cut into 1/2-inch cubes
- 4 slices thick-cut bacon — chopped

- 1 medium sweet potato — peeled and cut into 1/2 inch cubes (about 8 ounces)
- 1 medium onion — chopped
- 2 Granny Smith apples — peeled, cored and cut into 3/4 inch cubes
- 2 teaspoons chopped fresh thyme — or 1/2 teaspoon dried thyme
- 1/2 teaspoon black pepper
- 3 cups Brussels sprouts — trimmed and quartered (about 3/4 pound)
- 4 cloves garlic — minced (about 2 teaspoons)
- 1 teaspoon ground cinnamon
- 1 cup reduced-sodium chicken broth — divided

Instructions

- Heat oil in cast iron.
- Add the chicken, 1/2 teaspoon kosher salt, and black pepper. Cook. Transfer to plate.
- Add the chopped bacon and cook until crisp. Transfer the bacon to plate.
- Add Brussels sprouts, sweet potato, onion, and remaining 1/2 teaspoon salt. Cook.
- Stir in the apples, garlic, thyme, and cinnamon.
- Add the reserved chicken and remaining 1/2 cup broth. Cook until heated through, about 2 minutes. Stir in reserved bacon and serve warm.

Seared Sausage With Cabbage And Pink Lady Apples

Ingredients:

- 1 tbsp. olive oil
- 2 Pink Lady apples, halved
- 6 small sweet Italian sausage links (about 1 1/2 pounds total)
- 1/2 head red cabbage, cut into 1/2-inch-thick slices
- 1 c. fresh apple cider
- 1/2 red onion, sliced
- Kosher salt freshly ground black pepper
- 2 tbsp. fresh cider vinegar

Instructions:

- Heat oil in a large cast-iron skillet and add sausage.
- Reduce heat to medium and add apples. Scatter onion and cabbage around apples. Season with salt and pepper.
- Flip apples. Return sausage to skillet, nestling among vegetables.
- Add cider and vinegar. Simmer, rotating and turning sausages occasionally, until sausages are cooked through and apples are tender, 18 to 20 minutes.

Easy Unstuffed Bell Pepper Skillet

Ingredients

- 1 pound extra lean or lean ground turkey, chicken or bison
- 3 teaspoons ground cumin, divided
- 3 teaspoons chili powder, divided
- 3 teaspoons paprika, divided
- 1 teaspoon oregano, divided
- 1 red bell pepper, diced (1 cup)

- 1 yellow bell pepper, diced* (1 cup)
- 1 small onion, diced (1 cup)
- 2 cloves garlic, minced
- 2 small tomatoes, seeded and chopped
- 1 package SEEDS OF CHANGE™ Quinoa, Brown & Red Rice with Flaxseed (about 2 cups cooked rice)
- 1 lime, juiced (optional)
- 2 tablespoons chopped cilantro for garnish (optional)
- salt & pepper to taste

Instructions

- Spray a large skillet with cooking spray and heat over medium-high heat.
- Once pan is heated, add ground turkey to skillet and season with a dash of salt and pepper.
- Brown turkey, stirring occasionally. While turkey is browning, cook the SEEDS OF CHANGE™ Quinoa, Brown & Red Rice with Flaxseed for 90 seconds in the microwave and according to package instructions.
- When turkey is completely browned, add 2 tsp cumin, 2 tsp chili powder, 2 tsp paprika and 1/2 tsp oregano; stirring to combine.
- Remove turkey from skillet and set aside on a plate.
- Spray skillet again with cooking spray and add the pepper and onion to cook for about 3-5 mins and until soft, add garlic, tomatoes and the remainder of seasonings; continue to stir and cook for about 2 mins and until all veggies have softened.
- Add the turkey back into the veggies along with cooked SEEDS OF CHANGE™ Quinoa, Brown & Red Rice with Flaxseed.

- Squeeze lime juice over the mixture and stir everything together. Taste and season with salt & pepper or other seasonings to taste. Garnish with chopped cilantro and enjoy!

Sloppy Joe Tater Tot Casserole Recipe

Ingredients

- 2 cloves garlic, minced
- 1 pound ground beef, or turkey
- 8 ounces tomato sauce
- 1/2 cup ketchup
- 2 tablespoons brown sugar
- 2 tablespoons Worcestershire sauce
- 1 teaspoon prepared mustard
- 1/2 teaspoon garlic powder
- 1/4 teaspoon onion powder
- Freshly ground black pepper, to taste
- 1 can (15-ounces)pinto beans, rinsed & drained
- 1 1/2 cups grated sharp cheddar cheese, divided
- 1 bag (16-ounces)frozen tater tots

Instructions

- Set a 12-inch oven-safe skillet over medium-low heat. Add a few drops of extra-virgin olive oil, and saute the garlic for a minute or two until just fragrant and very light golden brown. Add the ground beef, increase heat to medium/medium high, and cook until no longer pink, breaking apart and stirring as the meat cooks. Drain the grease from the meat.

- While the meat is browning, arrange the oven rack in the center position, preheat the oven to 425°F, and prepare the sauce. In a large measuring cup, combine the tomato sauce, ketchup, brown sugar, Worcestershire sauce, mustard, garlic powder, onion powder, and freshly ground black pepper, to taste. Pour the sauce over the browned meat, stir to combine, and mix in the pinto beans. Simmer for 5 to 10 minutes until heated through and slightly thickened, stirring occasionally.

- Smooth the sloppy joe mixture in the skillet and sprinkle with 1 cup of the grated cheddar. Arrange the frozen tater tots in a single layer on top. Sprinkle with the remaining cheese and bake for 25 to 30 minutes or until the cheese is melted and the tater tots are browned.

20-Minute Skillet Tuscan Tortellini

INGREDIENTS
- 2 TB olive oil
- 1 green bell pepper, seeded and chopped
- 1 small onion, chopped
- 4 cloves garlic, chopped
- 1 lb bulk Italian sausage (no casings)
- 1 1/2 cups tomato-based pasta sauce
- 1 (14oz) can Italian diced tomatoes, with juices
- 1/2 cup chicken or vegetable broth

- 1/2 cup half and half
- 19 oz frozen cheese tortellini
- 3 cups baby spinach, torn to bite size
- freshly ground black pepper
- freshly shaved/shredded Parmesan cheese

Instructions

- In a very large skillet, heat oil over medium heat until hot. Add bell pepper, onion, and garlic. Stir constantly until fragrant, 30 seconds. Push mixture to the edges of pan and add sausage into the center of pan. Cook and break up sausage; once it's half-cooked, stir together with the vegetable mixture and continue cooking until browned.

- Add pasta sauce, tomatoes with juices, chicken or veggie broth, and half/half. Stir and bring to a simmer. Add frozen tortellini, stirring to submerge tortellini in the sauce. Cover and simmer until tender, about 7-8 minutes. Remove from heat. Add spinach and stir just until wilted. Add 1/4 tsp freshly ground black pepper (or to taste.) Serve immediately with freshly shaved/shredded Parmesan cheese.

Skillet Scalloped Potatoes

Ingredients

- 6 medium Yukon Gold potatoes, peeled and thinly sliced
- 3 tablespoons unsalted butter
- 3 tablespoons all purpose flour
- 1 1/2 cups milk

- 1 1/2 – 2 cups shredded Gruyere cheese
- 2 cloves garlic, minced
- 1 sprig thyme
- Salt and pepper, to taste

Instructions

- Preheat oven to 400 degrees F.
- Heat a 9 inch skillet over medium heat. Add the butter and reduce heat to low. Once the butter melts, add in the flour and whisk for 30 seconds. Add in the garlic, thyme, a pinch of salt and pepper, and whisk in the milk until smooth. Remove the skillet from the heat and pour the milk mixture into a separate bowl.
- Arrange the sliced potatoes in the skillet in an overlapping spiral pattern. Season each layer with a bit of salt and pepper, and sprinkle cheese between every layer of the potatoes.
- Pour the milk mixture back over the potatoes and then cover the top layer of potatoes with the remaining cheese.
- Cover with foil and bake for 1 hour. Remove the foil and bake for 5-10 minutes until top is golden.
- Let cool for 5-10 minutes and then serve!

Schmaltz-Refried Pinto Beans

Ingredients

- 3 ounces slab bacon, sliced ¼ inch thick

- 1 large onion, chopped
- 4 garlic cloves, chopped
- 1 dried chile de árbol, seeds removed, crushed, or ¼ teaspoon crushed red pepper flakes
- ½ teaspoon ground cumin
- 1½ cups dried pinto beans, soaked overnight
- Kosher salt, freshly ground pepper
- ⅓ cup schmaltz (chicken fat)
- 1 teaspoon (or more) apple cider vinegar

Instructions

- Cook bacon in a large saucepan over medium heat, turning often, until browned and lightly crisped, 8–10 minutes. Add onion and garlic and cook, stirring occasionally, until soft, 8–10 minutes. Add chile de árbol and cumin and cook, stirring occasionally, until fragrant, about 1 minute. Add beans and 4 cups water. Bring to a boil, reduce heat, and cover. Simmer, stirring occasionally and adding more water if needed to keep beans just covered, until beans are tender and beginning to fall apart, 1½–2 hours. Season with salt and pepper and let sit 30 minutes to absorb seasoning.
- Heat schmaltz in a pot or skillet over medium. Add beans and their cooking liquid and cook, mashing with a potato masher, until beans are nearly smooth and very thick, about 5 minutes. Stir in vinegar. Taste and adjust seasoning with salt and pepper and more vinegar, if desired. Thin with water if needed to loosen just before serving.

Poultry

Chicken Fajitas

Ingredients:
Marinade:

- 1 clove mince garlic
- 1½ teaspoons ground cumin
- 1½ teaspoons season salt
- ½ teaspoon crushed red pepper
- 2 tablespoons lime juice, fresh
- 1½ pounds chicken, sliced into strip
- ½ teaspoon chili powder
- 1 tablespoon olive oil

Fajita:

- ½ cup sliced onion
- 1 cup sliced red bell pepper
- ½ cup chopped green onion
- 8 large flour tortillas, warmed
- 3-4 tablespoons olive oil

Instructions:

- **Marinade:** Combine all ingredients. Marinate chicken strips for at least 2 hours.
- **Fajita:** Fry onions and peppers in oil until lightly browned; remove from pan. Sauté chicken. Toss in vegetables; and then spoon into flour tortillas.

La Paix Herb Farm's Rosemary Chicken

Ingredients:

- 4 chicken breasts, skinless
- 3 tablespoons butter
- Salt and pepper
- 1 cup white (Chardonnay, Pinot Grigio) or Rose wine
- 5 garlic cloves, chopped or pressed
- 1 green pepper cut into strips
- 1 tablespoon dried rosemary or
- 1½ cups mushrooms (shiitake preferred)
- 1 cup Mozzarella cheese, grated
- 4 fresh sprigs

Instructions:

- Preheat oven to 350°F.
- Cover bottom of iron chicken fryer skillet.
- Add chicken; fry.
- When breasts are cooked, add wine, garnish with mushrooms and peppers.
- Sprinkle rosemary in sauce and over chicken.
- Place chicken fryer in preheated oven and heat 30 minutes.

Simmered Tuscan Chicken

Ingredients:

- 1 pound chicken breast, boneless, skinless, 1" cubes

- 2 tablespoons olive oil
- 2 garlic cloves, minced
- 1 medium red bell pepper, diced
- 1 pound cut green beans, fresh or frozen
- 1 teaspoon dried basil
- 4 medium potatoes, ½" cubes (about 4 cups)
- 1 27-ounce jar marinara pasta sauce
- Salt and pepper to taste

Instructions:
- In a cast iron fry chicken with garlic in olive oil until chicken is lightly browned.
- Add potatoes and peppers.
- Add pasta sauce, green beans, basil, salt and pepper; bring to a boil.
- Cooking time is 40 minutes.

www.ingramcontent.com/pod-product-compliance
Lightning Source LLC
Chambersburg PA
CBHW071455070526
44578CB00001B/349